Paella Recipes

An Easy Paella Cookbook with Delicious Paella Recipes

By
BookSumo Press

Published by
http://www.booksumo.com

LEGAL NOTES

Table of Contents

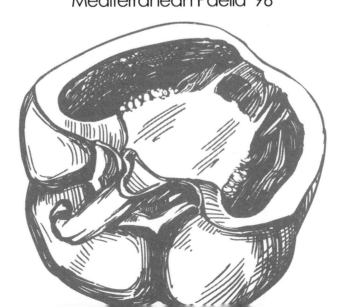

Paella
Romano

Prep Time: 35mins
Total Time:1 hr 30 mins

Servings per Recipe: 2
Calories   784
Fat   20.1
Cholesterol   301
Sodium   980
Carbohydrates   73.5
Protein   53

Ingredients

2 tbsp. olive oil
1 onion, diced
1/2 tomato, diced
1 pinch salt
1/2 tbsp. smoked paprika
6 fresh green beans
1/2 C. canned butter beans, drained and rinsed
1/2 C. white rice
6 large shrimps
6 mussels

6 clams
1 C. white wine
2 C. seafood stock
1 pinch saffron threads
1 tsp. chopped rosemary
1 C. peas
5 baby squid, cut into rings and tentacles
1 lemon wedges
1 tbsp. chopped flat-leaf parsley

Directions

1. Pour olive oil into a non-stick pan and heat well. Toss in the tomato, onion, smoked paprika and salt and leave for 4 minutes until tender. Stir in the butter beans, romano beans and rice and cook for 4 minutes.

2. Lay the mussels, shrimp and clams on top of the rice. Stir in seafood stock, white wine, rosemary and saffron threads and allow the mixture to simmer over a low heat.

3. Flip the shellfish and cook for 6 minutes until the shrimp turn pink in color. Transfer the mussels, clams and shrimp to a bowl and keep aside.

4. Add the peas, uncover and allow the mixture to simmer for about 26 minutes until the rice is cooked and the mixture becomes dry.

5. Add the squid and place the mussels, clams and shrimp in the pan once again. Allow to cook for another 4 minutes. Serve garnished with chopped parsley and lemon wedges.

6. Enjoy.

CORDOBA
One Pot

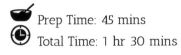

Prep Time: 45 mins
Total Time: 1 hr 30 mins

Servings per Recipe: 6
Calories   524
Fat   18.2
Cholesterol   106
Sodium   1162
Carbohydrates   56.6
Protein   28.8

Ingredients

4 tbsp. olive oil
1 onion, chopped
2 cloves garlic, minced
1 red bell pepper, chopped
4 ounces Spanish cured spiced pork sausage, diced and casing discarded
2 skinless, boneless chicken breast halves, cubed
1 (12 ounce) package uncooked Arborio rice
5 C. chicken broth
1/2 C. white wine

1 sprig thyme
1 pinch saffron
salt
ground black pepper
2 squid, cleaned and cut into pieces
2 tomatoes, seeded and chopped
1/2 C. frozen green peas
12 large shrimp, peeled and deveined
1 pound mussels, cleaned and debearded
1/4 C. chopped Italian flat leaf parsley
8 slices lemon

Directions

1. Pour olive oil into a skillet and heat well. Sauté garlic, onion and pepper for about 3 minutes. Stir in sausage, rice and chicken and cook for 4 minutes. Fold in 3 1/2 C. of stock, thyme, wine and saffron. Adjust seasonings with salt and pepper. Allow the mixture to boil, reduce heat and allow to simmer for 16 minutes.
2. Check the rice and see whether it is cooked adequately. If the rice is not cooked properly add about half a C. of stock. Combine well and continue to cook. Add more stock if required: add up to 5 C. in total.
3. Add the tomatoes, squid and peas and leave for 3 minutes. Spread mussels and prawns on top. Use a foil to cover and leave for 6 minutes.
4. Take out the foil cover and sprinkle parsley on top. Serve garnished with wedges of lemon.
5. Enjoy.

Lulu's
Award Winning Paella

Prep Time: 3o mins
Total Time:1 hr 10 mins

Servings per Recipe: 6
Calories	814
Fat	29.9
Cholesterol	211
Sodium	770
Carbohydrates	87.4
Protein	47.2

Ingredients

1/2 C. olive oil
1 1/4 pounds chicken thighs
1/2 C. onion, diced
2 cloves garlic, chopped
1/2 green bell pepper, diced
1/2 red bell pepper, diced
1/4 pound calamari rings
1/4 pound small shrimp, peeled and deveined
1 tsp. salt
2 tsps. saffron threads
1 (14 ounce) can crushed tomatoes

1/2 C. peas
3 C. long grain rice
6 C. water
6 large clams in shell, scrubbed
6 jumbo shrimp in shells
6 large sea scallops
6 wedges lemon

Directions

1. Pour olive oil into a pan and heat until it smokes. Lay the chicken pieces skin side facing downwards and leave for 6 minutes until slightly brown on each side. Leave aside.
2. Toss in onion and garlic and leave until the onion becomes tender for 1 minute. Stir in bell peppers, small shrimp and calamari and leave for 2 minutes. Add salt, tomatoes, saffron, rice, peas and water and mix well. Toss in the chicken pieces and allow the mixture to simmer for 16 minutes; stir often to ensure the rice is not sticky. Decorate the rice with clams and jumbo shrimp. Lower the heat to medium low, cover with lid and allow to simmer for 12 minutes. Place scallops on the rice, cover and cook until the rice is cooked and the scallops opaque in color for 6 minutes. Serve garnished with lemon wedges. Enjoy.

PAELLA
Festival

Prep Time: 10 mins
Total Time: 1 hr

Servings per Recipe: 4
Calories	308
Fat	4.6
Cholesterol	0
Sodium	1103
Carbohydrates	58.8
Protein	8.2

Ingredients

2 C. boiling water
1 C. white rice
1 tbsp. olive oil
1 onion, chopped
3 cloves garlic, minced
1 green bell pepper, sliced
1 red bell pepper, sliced
1 tomato, diced
2 C. vegetable broth

1 tbsp. paprika
1 tsp. salt
1 tsp. ground turmeric
1 C. peas
1 C. drained and quartered canned artichoke hearts

Directions

1. Pour boiling water into a saucepan and add the rice; leave for 22 minutes. Drain the rice using a colander.
2. Pour olive oil into a pan and heat well. Sauté the onion and garlic for about 6 minutes until the onion becomes soft. Toss in tomato, red bell pepper and green bell pepper and cook for 4 minutes until the peppers become soft.
3. Fold in the rice and vegetable broth into the pan and allow the mixture to boil. Lower the heat and allow the mixture to simmer for a few minutes. Stir in paprika, turmeric and salt, cover with lid and cook for 22 minutes until the rice is cooked. Toss in artichoke hearts and peas and leave for 2 minutes more.
4. Enjoy.

Occidental
Paella

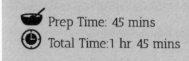

Prep Time: 45 mins
Total Time:1 hr 45 mins

Servings per Recipe: 8
Calories   591
Fat   21.8
Cholesterol   153
Sodium   1032
Carbohydrates   54
Protein   42

Ingredients

2 1/2 C. uncooked white rice
6 C. chicken stock, divided
3 cloves garlic
1 tsp. chopped parsley
1/2 tsp. curry powder
5 saffron threads
salt and ground black pepper
1/4 C. olive oil
1 onion, diced

1 (3 pound) whole chicken, cut into pieces
2 C. peeled and deveined small shrimp, diced
6 small lobster tails
1/2 pound clams in shell, scrubbed
1 (8 ounce) jar mushrooms, drained
1 C. green peas
1 (2 ounce) can mussels

Directions

1. Wash the rice with cold water; drain using a colander and leave aside. Pour chicken stock into a pot and allow the mixture to boil, lower the heat, cover with lid to maintain the warmth.

2. Place the garlic, curry powder, parsley, salt, saffron threads, 1/2 C. of hot chicken stock and black pepper in a mortar and pestle and pound until a liquid is formed; set the liquid aside.

3. Pour olive oil into a skillet and heat well. Sauté the onion in the warm oil until a slight brown in color. Fold in the chicken, lobster, shrimp and clams; leave to cook for 12 minutes until the chicken is cooked. Add the kept aside liquid to the chicken mixture.

4. Toss in the rice and the hot chicken stock and allow the mixture to simmer for 16 minutes. Stir in the peas, mushrooms and mussels, combine twice and leave to simmer for 12 minutes. Transfer from heat; cover with lid and leave for 8 minutes until rice is flaky and soft.

5. Enjoy.

MIDNIGHT
Paella

Prep Time: 10 mins
Total Time: 40 mins

Servings per Recipe: 8

Calories	253
Fat	8.9
Cholesterol	106
Sodium	864
Carbohydrates	24.4
Protein	14.8

Ingredients

2 C. water

1/2 pound smoked sausage, halved lengthwise and sliced

1 (14.5 ounce) can diced tomatoes, undrained

1/2 C. chopped onion

1 tsp. dried parsley flakes

1 (6.9 ounce) package ZATARAIN'S Yellow Rice

1 pound large shrimp, peeled and deveined

1 C. frozen peas

Directions

1. Place sausage, onion, tomatoes and parsley in a pan. Add water and bring to a boil.
2. Add the rice, allow to boil and lower the heat, cover with lid and allow to simmer for 16 minutes.
3. Toss in peas and shrimp to the rice. Cover with lid and cook for 16 minutes until the rice is cooked and tender.
4. Transfer from heat and leave for 5 minutes to come to room temperature.
5. Enjoy.

Paella
Mexicana

Prep Time: 10 mins
Total Time: 55 mins

Servings per Recipe: 8

Calories	368
Fat	22.7
Cholesterol	74
Sodium	1244
Carbohydrates	12.2
Protein	28.6

Ingredients

1 pound chorizo sausage
1 skinless, boneless chicken breast
3 C. cauliflower rice, divided
1 medium onion, diced
1 large yellow bell pepper, seeded and chopped
1 pinch salt
ground black pepper
3 cloves garlic, minced
1 (14.5 ounce) can Hunt's Diced Tomatoes

2 bay leaves
1 1/2 tsps. thyme leaves
1/2 tsp. crushed saffron threads
1/2 tsp. dried basil
1/2 C. water
2 tbsp. tomato paste
2 cubes chicken bouillon
1 C. frozen peas
3 frozen tilapia fillets

Directions

1. Heat a non-stick skillet and cook the sausage for 6 minutes breaking up into pieces. Stir in the chicken and leave until nicely browned. Remove the mixture and place on a serving dish.

2. Lower the heat and mix in 2 C. of cauliflower rice; cook for 6 minutes until slightly brown. Stir in the onion and bell pepper. Adjust seasoning by adding a bit of salt and pepper. Toss in the garlic and cook for 3 minutes.

3. Add the canned tomatoes into the skillet. Fold in the thyme leaves, bay leaves, basil and saffron and combine well. Place the chicken and sausage mixture once again in the skillet. Pour water, bouillon and tomato paste; mix all ingredients together. Allow the mixture to boil, lower the heat, cover with lid and allow to simmer for 16 minutes.

4. Take out the lid and add the peas and the balance C. of cauliflower rice. Lay the tilapia filets on top of the rice mix, cover and allow to cook for another 12 minutes. With a spatula gently break the fillets and combine with the paella.

5. Enjoy..

PAELLA
Americana

Prep Time: 15 mins
Total Time: 45 mins

Servings per Recipe: 8
Calories   381
Fat   8.2
Cholesterol   144
Sodium   1161
Carbohydrates   40.7
Protein   32.9

Ingredients

1 tbsp. vegetable oil
2 C. uncooked regular long-grain white rice
4 C. Chicken Stock, heated
1 C. Thick & Chunky Salsa
1 tsp. ground turmeric
1 (16 ounce) package turkey kielbasa, sliced
12 ounces frozen peeled and deveined

cooked shrimp, thawed
1 (10 ounce) package refrigerated cooked chicken breast strips

Directions

1. Pour oil into a pan and heat well. Fold in the rice, stir constantly and allow to cook for 32 seconds. Add the salsa, stock and turmeric and allow the mixture to boil. Lower the heat, cover with lid and allow to cook for 16 minutes.

2. Fold in the turkey, chicken and shrimp. Replace the lid and cook for 6 minutes until the liquid becomes dry and the rice becomes tender.

3. Enjoy.

New Hampshire
Paella

🥣 Prep Time: 45 mins

🕐 Total Time: 1 hr 35 mins

Servings per Recipe: 8
Calories	409
Fat	6.8
Cholesterol	103
Sodium	803
Carbohydrates	52.9
Protein	33.4

Ingredients

2 tbsp. olive oil
16 head-on medium shrimp
1 red onion, diced
2 tsps. minced garlic
2 C. Arborio rice
5 1/2 C. hot fish stock
1/4 tsp. saffron threads
1 1/2 tsps. smoked paprika
1 tsp. lemon zest
1 tbsp. chopped oregano
sea salt
16 mussels, scrubbed and debearded
1 pound red snapper fillets, cut into pieces
1/4 pound medium shrimp, peeled and deveined
1 (10 ounce) cooked lobster tail, sliced
2 tomatoes, seeded and diced
2 lemons wedges

Directions

1. Pour olive oil into a pan and heat well. Toss in the shrimp and leave until the shrimp is slightly browned on the outside, the shrimp should be raw in the middle. Transfer the shrimp and keep aside.

2. Lower the heat and add the garlic and onion and leave until the onion becomes soft. Fold in Arborio rice and allow to coat well with the oil. Add the fish stock, saffron, lemon zest, paprika and oregano. Allow the mixture to simmer and add sea salt. Lower the heat, remove lid and cook for 16 minutes ensuring to stir occasionally.

3. Lay the mussels on the rice, cover with lid and allow to simmer for 6 minutes. Add the deveined shrimp and red snapper into the rice, cover with lid allow to simmer for 12 minutes.

4. Stir in the lobster and sprinkle diced tomatoes on top. Cover with lid and cook for 6 minutes more until the rice is cooked.

5. Serve garnished with lemon wedges. Enjoy.

BOXED
Paella

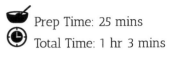 Prep Time: 25 mins

Total Time: 1 hr 3 mins

Servings per Recipe: 4

Calories	247
Fat	12
Cholesterol	173
Sodium	647
Carbohydrates	14.1
Protein	20.5

Ingredients

2 C. water
1 (7 ounce) box Spanish yellow rice mix
3 tbsp. olive oil, divided
1/2 C. diced onion
1 pound uncooked medium shrimp, peeled and deveined
1 green bell pepper, diced
1 red bell pepper, diced

1 tbsp. sweet and spicy seafood seasoning
1/2 C. parsley

Directions

1. Pour water into a pot and allow to boil. Stir in 1 tbsp of olive oil and the rice mix and leave for 2 minutes. Cover with lid and lower the heat and allow to simmer until the liquid is fully absorbed for about 26 minutes.
2. Heat the balance olive oil in a pan. Temper the onion until soft for 3 minutes. Toss in green bell pepper, shrimp, red bell pepper and seafood seasoning. Leave for 6 minutes until the shrimp becomes opaque.
3. Serve rice onto plates and top up with the shrimp mixture. Serve garnished with parsley.
4. Enjoy.

Paella
in Tunisian Style

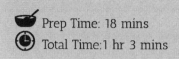 Prep Time: 18 mins

Total Time:1 hr 3 mins

Servings per Recipe: 6

Calories	519
Fat	16.8
Cholesterol	76
Sodium	707
Carbohydrates	55.8
Protein	30.3

Ingredients

1/4 C. olive oil
1 onion, chopped
1 roasted red pepper, chopped
2 cloves garlic, chopped
3 vine-ripened tomatoes, chopped
1 (8 ounce) salmon fillet, cut into pieces
5 ounces beef sausage, cut into pieces
6 C. vegetable broth, divided
1/2 C. white wine

1 tsp. ground cumin
salt and ground black pepper
12 shrimp, shelled and deveined
12 mussels, cleaned and debearded
2 (5.8 ounce) boxes couscous

Directions

1. Pour olive oil into a skillet and heat well. Sauté onion, garlic and roasted red pepper and leave for 5 minutes.
2. Add tomatoes, salmon and sausage and cook for 4 minutes.
3. Stir in 2 1/2 C. of broth and white wine into the skillet. Add salt, pepper and cumin and allow the mixture to boil.
4. Lower the heat and add the shrimp and leave for 4 minutes until the shrimp becomes pink. Transfer from heat, add the mussels and leave for about 6 minutes until the mussels open fully.
5. Pour the balance 3 1/2 C. of broth to a separate saucepan and allow to boil. Add couscous and combine well. Transfer from heat and leave for 6 minutes until the couscous absorbs the liquid.
6. Dish out couscous into bowls; drizzle the stew mixture on top.
7. Enjoy..

HOT TOMATO
Paella

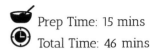

Prep Time: 15 mins
Total Time: 46 mins

Servings per Recipe: 10
Calories	246
Fat	4.7
Cholesterol	10
Sodium	594
Carbohydrates	42.4
Protein	8.6

Ingredients

1/2 pound turkey bacon, chopped
1 onion, chopped
2 pounds tomatillos, husked and chopped
1 (10 ounce) package frozen peas
1 bell pepper, chopped
3 jalapeno peppers, sliced
1 tsp. paprika
1 pinch saffron

2 C. uncooked white rice
4 C. chicken broth
1 bunch cilantro, chopped

Directions

1. Place a non-stick pan on stovetop and heat well. Sauté the bacon and leave for about 6 minutes.
2. Transfer the bacon from the pan with a non-stick spoon, keeping the bacon fat in the pan.
3. Toss in the onion to the pan and cook until soft for 6 minutes. Stir in peas, tomatillos and bell pepper into the pan; allow to cook until soft for 6 minutes.
4. Fold in paprika, jalapeno peppers, rice and saffron into the pan; add broth.
5. Cover with lid and cook until the rice is done for about 38 minutes. Toss in the kept aside bacon and cilantro and combine well.
6. Enjoy..

Venetian
Paella

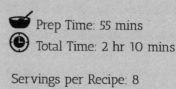

Prep Time: 55 mins
Total Time: 2 hr 10 mins

Servings per Recipe: 8

Calories	908
Fat	38.9
Cholesterol	260
Sodium	832
Carbohydrates	78.2
Protein	59.9

Ingredients

1/2 pound green beans, trimmed

1/2 C. minced parsley

2 cloves garlic, minced

1 saffron thread

sea salt

1/2 C. extra-virgin olive oil

1 1/4 pounds pork spareribs, cut into pieces

1/2 pound rabbit, cut into pieces

1 (2.5 pound) whole chicken, cut into pieces

1/2 pound squid, cut into pieces

2 large tomatoes, peeled and chopped

1 onion, chopped

1 red bell pepper, seeded and sliced into strips

2 1/2 C. short-grain rice

1/2 pound frozen peas

1 lemon, juiced

4 C. hot chicken stock

1 pound medium shrimp, peeled and deveined

1 pound mussels, cleaned and debearded

ground pepper

1 lemon wedges

4 sprigs flat-leaf parsley

Directions

1. Pour water to a saucepan, add a pinch of salt and allow the liquid to boil. Toss in fresh green beans and cook without a lid for 4 minutes. Drain the excess liquid with the use of a colander and insert the green beans into ice water. Drain again with the use of a colander.

2. Place garlic, parsley, salt and saffron in a bowl and form into a smooth paste.

3. Pour oil into a pan and heat well. Toss in rabbit and pork and cook for 17 minutes until both sides are nicely browned. Remove the meat and place in a serving plate.

4. Add the chicken for a few minutes and remove from the pan. Toss in squid into the pan and allow to cook for 6 minutes. Remove the squid and place the squid in the serving dish.

5. Toss in onion, tomato and red pepper into the pan, and allow to cook until tender for 4 minutes. Add the pork, chicken, rabbit and squid to the pan once again.

6. Fold in the garlic paste, rice peas, green beans and lemon juice into the pan. Cook for 4 minutes until the peas become soft.

7. Stir in the chicken stock into the pan and allow the mixture to boil. Lower the heat and allow to simmer for about 12 minutes until the rice is tender and cooked. Add the mussels and shrimp and leave for 12 minutes until the shrimp is no longer pink.

8. Remove the mussels which do not open during the cooking process. Adjust seasonings with pepper.

9. Transfer from heat and leave covered with lid for 12 minutes for the rice to absorb the excess liquid. Serve garnished with parsley sprigs and lemon wedges. Enjoy.

BIG
World Paella

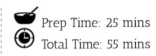 Prep Time: 25 mins
Total Time: 55 mins

Servings per Recipe: 4	
Calories	427
Fat	26.9
Cholesterol	26
Sodium	2196
Carbohydrates	32
Protein	18.1

Ingredients

1 head cauliflower, broken into florets
2 tbsp. hot water
1/2 tsp. saffron threads
1/4 C. extra-virgin olive oil, divided
3 links sweet Italian chicken sausage, diced
1 large zucchini, chopped
1 yellow onion, chopped
1 carrot, grated

2 cloves garlic, minced
1/4 tsp. ground cayenne pepper
1 (15 ounce) can artichokes, drained
3 C. chicken stock
sea salt
1/2 tsp. ground black pepper
1 1/2 C. snow peas

Directions

1. Insert the florets into a food processor and process until the mixture becomes similar to rice in consistency.
2. Place saffron and hot water in a bowl and leave for 4 minutes.
3. Pour 2 tbsp of olive oil into a skillet and heat well.
4. Toss in sausage and allow to cook for 6 minutes until nicely browned on all sides.
5. Stir in onion and zucchini and allow to cook for 4 minutes. Fold in saffron mixture, garlic, carrot and cayenne pepper and leave for 2 minutes.
6. Add the processed rice and artichokes into the skillet and allow to cook for 4 minutes until soft. Stir in stock; adjust seasonings with salt and pepper.
7. Allow the mixture to boil; lower the heat and leave for 12 minutes until the liquid is fully absorbed. Add snow peas; and leave for 6 minutes.
8. Take out the skillet from the heat and add the balance 2 tbsp of olive oil on the surface.
9. Enjoy.

Paella
Spaghetti

Prep Time: 30 mins
Total Time: 1 hr 25 mins

Servings per Recipe: 4
Calories   636
Fat   15.5
Cholesterol   17
Sodium   895
Carbohydrates   101
Protein   23.5

Ingredients

3 C. chicken stock
2 cloves garlic, minced
1 pinch saffron
1 C. pancetta bacon, diced
2 tbsp. olive oil, divided
1/2 C. diced carrots
1/2 C. frozen artichoke hearts, thawed
1/2 C. green beans
2 C. diced white onion

salt and black pepper
2 C. diced tomatoes
1 (16 ounce) package spaghetti, broken into pieces

Directions

1. Place garlic, chicken stock and saffron in a small pot. Warm the pot slightly until hot. Cover with lid and maintain the warmth so the saffron will continue to infuse.

2. Cook the bacon in a non-stick pan until the fat is rendered out and the bacon is cooked for about 12 minutes. Transfer the bacon from the pan and leave aside. Remove the fat from the pan and fold in 1 tbsp of olive oil. Sauté the artichoke hearts, carrots and green beans until the veggies are soft. Transfer the vegetables from the pan and leave aside. Pour the balance 1 tbsp of olive oil into the pan and sauté the onion. Adjust seasonings with salt and pepper and leave for 12 minutes until the onion becomes soft. Stir in tomatoes and leave for 22 minutes until the mixture forms a paste.

3. Lay the onion mixture in the bottom of the pan; sprinkle spaghetti pieces on top. Fold in the saffron infuse to cover the spaghetti, lay the bacon and vegetables on top.

4. Stir in more saffron broth if needed. Allow the mixture to simmer, lower the heat and cook until the spaghetti becomes tender for about 16 minutes.

5. Enjoy.

BATON
Rouge Paella

Prep Time: 30 mins
Total Time: 1 hr 15 mins

Servings per Recipe: 6
Calories	757
Fat	30.5
Cholesterol	277
Sodium	1867
Carbohydrates	62.8
Protein	54.6

Ingredients

2 tbsp. olive oil
4 chicken leg quarters
2 (8 ounce) packages dirty rice mix
5 C. water
2 pounds whole cooked crawfish, peeled
3/4 medium shrimp, peeled and deveined
1/2 pound andouille sausage, sliced into rounds

2 C. sliced mushrooms
1 large green bell pepper, chopped
1 large sweet onion, chopped
3 cloves garlic, minced

Directions

1. Pour olive oil into a skillet and heat well. Sauté the chicken legs until both sides are nicely browned.
2. Toss in rice mix, water, shrimp, crawfish, mushrppendixooms, sausage, onion, bell pepper and garlic.
3. Allow the mixture to boil, and combine the mixture well.
4. Lower the heat, cover with lid and cook for 32 minutes until the rice becomes cooked and tender.
5. Enjoy.

Guyanese Paella

Prep Time: 20 mins
Total Time: 50mins

Servings per Recipe: 4
Calories	555.9
Fat	15.0g
Cholesterol	139.4mg
Sodium	860.0mg
Carbohydrates	61.0g
Protein	42.1g

Ingredients

2 tsps. sesame oil
125 g shallots, peeled and sliced
20 g gingerroot, grated
2 garlic cloves, chopped
400 g chicken breasts
salt and pepper
250 g orzo pasta
1 1/2 tsps. smoked paprika
600 ml chicken stock

225 - 250 g prawns, cooked
1/4 C. lemon juice
3 tsps. soy sauce
1/3 C. coriander leaves, chopped

Directions

1. Slice the chicken into 3cm pieces.
2. Pour sesame oil into a skillet and heat well.
3. Sauté shallots, garlic and ginger until soft for a few minutes.
4. Toss in the chicken pieces to the skillet, adjust seasonings by adding salt and pepper and cook until nicely browned on each side.
5. Stir in orzo and allow to coat with sesame oil.
6. Adjust seasonings with paprika and pour the stock over the ingredients. All the stock may not be required at once.
7. Leave to simmer for about 16 minutes. Add more stock if necessary.
8. Stir in the prawns, soy and lemon juice and combine well. Adjust seasonings if required.
9. Leave for 6 minutes in the skillet, cover and allow the chicken to become tender.
10. Add the chopped coriander and serve with more leaves.
11. Enjoy.

TRADITIONAL
Paella in Portuguese Style

Prep Time: 12 mins
Total Time: 57 mins

Servings per Recipe: 6
Calories	607.4
Fat	18.4g
Cholesterol	193.6mg
Sodium	1314.2mg
Carbohydrates	65.4g
Protein	42.0g

Ingredients

1/4 C. olive oil
3 chicken breasts, cubed
1/2 tsp. salt
1/4 tsp. pepper
1 large Spanish onion, chopped
1 green pepper, diced into pieces
4 cloves garlic, chopped
2 tsps. Spanish paprika
1 tbsp. fresh thyme
1 lb. shrimp, shelled and deveined
2 C. Arborio rice
1 C. chopped tomatoes
5 C. chicken broth
1/2 tsp. saffron thread
1 C. lima beans
1/2 C. roasted red pepper, strips
1/4 C. chopped parsley
12 clams in shell
lemon wedge
green onion

Directions

1. Pour 3 tbsp oil into a pan and heat well.
2. Toss in the chicken and sauté for 5 minutes on each side until a slight brown in color.
3. Transfer the chicken into a dish and adjust seasonings with salt and pepper.
4. Fold in peppers and onions into the pan and temper for 3 minutes.
5. Add paprika, garlic and thyme and leave for 1 minute.
6. Toss in shrimp and leave until pink in color.
7. Pour 1 tbsp oil if required.
8. Add rice into the pan; stir and temper for 4 minutes until evenly coated in oil.
9. Add the tomatoes.
10. Pour the saffron and stock into the rice mixture and allow the mixture to boil for 3 minutes.
11. Lower the heat to medium.
12. Transfer the chicken once again into the pan with rice.
13. Remove lid and leave to cook for 16 minutes.
14. Allow the mixture to bubble.
15. Add lima beans, shrimp, clams and red peppers and cook for 12 minutes.
16. Transfer from heat and keep covered for 12 minutes.
17. Sprinkle parsley on top and serve garnished with green onions and lemon wedges.
18. Enjoy.

2 Brother's
Paella

Prep Time: 1 hr
Total Time: 1 hr 45 mins

Servings per Recipe: 8
Calories   887.3
Fat   28.6g
Cholesterol   344.9mg
Sodium   1820.9mg
Carbohydrates   76.8g
Protein   74.1g

Ingredients

2 1/2 lbs. chicken parts
1/4 C. olive oil
1 medium onion, diced
4 garlic cloves, minced
2 tsps. salt
ground pepper
1/2 tsp. paprika
1 large red bell pepper, roasted, peeled, seeded, and diced

1/2 C. sliced green onion
1 lb. squid, cleaned, sacs cut into rings
1/2 tsp. saffron thread
1 lb. large raw shrimp, peeled and deveined
3 C. short-grain rice
6 C. warm chicken stock
1 1/2 lbs. small live clams
1 C. frozen peas

Directions

1. Slice each breast half into 3 parts and each thigh into 4 parts.
2. Pour the oil into a skillet and heat well.
3. Sauté the onion and garlic for a few minutes.
4. Increase the heat when the onions begin to sizzle.
5. Stir in the chicken and allow to cook until slightly browned; sprinkle paprika, salt and pepper on the chicken.
6. Once the chicken is cooked transfer the pieces towards the outside of the skillet making room in the middle of the skillet.
7. Stir in the squid, green onion, peppers and the balance salt; crumble the saffron and add to the chicken. Fold in the rice and leave for 2 minutes to coat evenly with oil.
8. Pour the hot stock to within 1" of the rim of the skillet. You may not require all the stock.
9. Spread the shrimp on top; place the clams and mussels in a circle around the edge, hinged side facing downwards.
10. Allow the mixture to simmer for about 22 minutes until the rice becomes tender; sprinkle the peas on top midway during the cooking time. Enjoy.

CAJUN
Paella

Prep Time: 1 hr 30 mins
Total Time: 2 hr

Servings per Recipe: 8
Calories	809.6
Fat	47.1g
Cholesterol	235.1mg
Sodium	1305.5mg
Carbohydrates	40.1g
Protein	52.0g

Ingredients

1/4 C. olive oil
3 lbs. chicken, cut-up, bone-in
1/4 C. water
1 tsp. oregano
1 large onion, chopped
2 garlic cloves, minced
1/2 tbsp. parsley, minced
1 seeded jalapeno, minced
2 C. long-grain rice
1/2 tsp. turmeric

3 tbsp. butter
4 C. chicken broth
scant 1/2 tsp. salt
1 lb. shrimp, cooked and cleaned
1/2 lb. smoked sausage, sliced
1/4 lb. ham, diced, optional
salt and pepper

Directions

1. Rub the chicken with salt and pepper.
2. Pour olive oil into a skillet and heat well; toss in the chicken and keep until a slight brown in color.
3. Stir in oregano and 1/4 C. water; cover with lid and leave for 35 minutes until the chicken becomes tender.
4. Take out the cooked chicken and leave aside.
5. Add the onion and garlic to the skillet and sauté until soft. Add the jalapeno and the parsley.
6. Heat the butter and allow to melt in a separate saucepan with lid; cover and leave on a low heat for 18 minutes.
7. Stir in garlic and onion and combine well.
8. Arrange the rice, shrimp, chicken, ham and sausage in layers in an ovenproof dish.Bake for 32 minutes at a temperature of 350F. Enjoy.

Butter
Bean Paella

Prep Time: 30 mins
Total Time: 2 hrs

Servings per Recipe: 8
Calories	31.3
Fat	82
Cholesterol	328
Sodium	87.3
Carbohydrates	34.2
Protein	31.3

Ingredients

1 tbsp. olive oil
1/2 (4 pound) whole chicken, cut into 6 pieces
1/2 (2 pound) rabbit, cleaned and cut into pieces
1 head garlic, cloves separated and peeled
1 tomato, chopped
1 (15.5 ounce) can butter beans
1/2 (10 ounce) package frozen green peas

1/2 (10 ounce) package frozen green beans
salt
1 tsp. mild paprika
1 pinch saffron threads
dried thyme
dried rosemary
4 C. uncooked white rice

Directions

1. Pour olive oil into a skillet and heat well. Toss in the rabbit, chicken and garlic and cook until a slight brown in color. Transfer the slightly browned meat into a side of the skillet; add tomato, peas and butter beans. Adjust seasonings with paprika and combine the mixture well.

2. Measure the water and pour into the skillet. Allow the mixture to boil, reduce heat and allow the mixture to simmer for about 1 hour and 10 minutes.

3. Add a pinch of salt and saffron for color yellow. If required add rosemary and thyme.

4. Fold in the rice, cover with lid, lower the heat and allow the mixture to simmer until the liquid dries up for about 22 minutes.

5. Enjoy.

BEACON
Hill Paella

 Prep Time: 45 mins

Total Time: 1 hr 15 mins

Servings per Recipe: 8

Calories	290.3
Fat	4.5g
Cholesterol	21.7mg
Sodium	220.5mg
Carbohydrates	47.6g
Protein	13.8g

Ingredients

1 white onion, medium dice
1 red bell pepper, medium dice
2 C. long grain rice
2 - 3 sausage links, cut across into rounds
1 (8 ounce) packages chicken tenders, cut across into pieces
15 - 20 medium shrimp, cleaned, uncooked
3 green onions, sliced across
1 C. frozen peas, steamed, drained
1 (32 ounce) boxes chicken stock
1 bay leaf
1 tbsp. saffron
2 - 3 garlic cloves, chopped
2 tsps. red pepper flakes
1 tbsp. paprika
1 - 3 tbsp. olive oil
1 - 2 tsp. salt and pepper
1 lemon wedges

Directions

1. Add the bay leaf and saffron into a saucepan and pour in the chicken stock. Allow the mixture to simmer.
2. Rub the chicken with salt, pepper and paprika,
3. Pour 1 1/2 tbsp olive oil into a skillet and temper the chicken until a slight brown on all sides. Remove the ingredients and transfer into a platter.
4. Toss in sausage to the skillet and allow to brown on all sides. Combine the sausage with the chicken whilst keeping any oil in the skillet.
5. Toss in onion, garlic, red bell pepper, salt and pepper into the skillet and temper for a few minutes until soft. Add more oil if required.
6. Stir in the rice and stir fry for 5 minutes.
7. Pour the chicken stock to the skillet, combine, lower the heat, cover with lid and allow to simmer for 12 minutes.
8. Add the chicken, shrimp and sausage. Sprinkle peas on top, keep the lid on and allow the mixture to simmer for 12 more minutes.
9. Transfer from heat, sprinkle green onions on top.
10. Serve with wedges of lemon.
11. Enjoy.

Italian
Paella

🍳 Prep Time: 5 mins
🕐 Total Time: 30 mins

Servings per Recipe: 5
Calories	603.9
Fat	12.8g
Cholesterol	351.8mg
Sodium	850.3mg
Carbohydrates	74.6g
Protein	43.2g

Ingredients

1 lb. shrimp
1 lb. squid
1 lb. mussels
2 C. short-grain rice
1 onion, minced
1 tbsp. tomato paste
1/2 green pepper
1/2 red pepper
2 garlic cloves, minced

3 tbsp. olive oil
1/2 tsp. saffron thread
salt
pepper
5 C. water

Directions

1. Pour olive oil into a skillet and heat well. Sauté the onion and garlic for 4 minutes.
2. Toss in the tomato paste and peppers and leave for 4 more minutes.
3. Stir in the rice, squids, saffron, salt and pepper and leave for 4 minutes.
4. Pour the warm water into the ingredients.
5. Stir in the balance olive oil.
6. Once the liquid is absorbed stir in the mussels and shrimps.
7. Stir occasionally and allow to cook for 12 more minutes.
8. Enjoy.

PAELLA
Maella

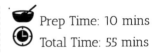 Prep Time: 10 mins

Total Time: 55 mins

Servings per Recipe: 4
Calories	412.4
Fat	11.6g
Cholesterol	0.0mg
Sodium	1202.0mg
Carbohydrates	71.5g
Protein	8.3g

Ingredients

3 tbsp. olive oil
1 large onion, diced
6 garlic cloves, minced
1/2 tsp. red chili pepper flakes
2 tsps. salt
1 tbsp. chili powder
1 tbsp. sweet paprika
2 tsps. oregano
1 large red pepper, chopped
1 large yellow pepper, chopped

4 medium tomatoes, ripe, chopped
1 1/4 C. Arborio rice
3 C. vegetable stock
1/2 lb. green beans, trimmed and sliced
into lengths
fresh ground pepper
1/2 bunch cilantro, chopped
1/2 bunch parsley, chopped
1 bunch scallion, minced
cheddar cheese

Directions

1. Pour olive oil into a skillet and heat well. Add onion and allow to cook until tender. Toss in chile flakes, garlic and 1 tsp salt and temper until the garlic becomes soft.

2. Stir in the balance salt, herbs, spices, tomatoes and peppers, cover with lid and allow to simmer for 12 minutes. Add the rice and allow to coat evenly.

3. Pour the water or stock to a saucepan, heat and pour the warm liquid into the skillet. Cover with lid and lower the heat.

4. Allow the rice to cook until tender for 32 minutes until the liquid has been fully absorbed. In the meantime, blanch or steam the beans until soft.

5. Stir in the beans to the skillet. Adjust seasonings with fresh herbs and cracked pepper.

6. Garnish with minced scallions and grated cheese and serve.

7. Enjoy.

American
Paella

Prep Time: 15 mins
Total Time: 55 mins

Servings per Recipe: 6
Calories	752.8
Fat	33.8g
Cholesterol	214.0mg
Sodium	1643.0mg
Carbohydrates	65.8g
Protein	44.2g

Ingredients

1 tbsp. olive oil
1 lb. chorizo sausage, sliced
1 large onion, diced
2 garlic cloves, minced
1 (1 ounce) packet vegetable soup mix
1/2 tsp. paprika
2 C. long-grain rice
4 C. low sodium chicken broth
1 (14 ounce) cans diced tomatoes, drained

1 C. frozen peas
1 lb. previously cooked frozen shrimp
pepper

Directions

1. Before you do anything set the oven to 400F. Pour oil into a skillet and heat well. Sauté the chorizo and leave for 6 minutes until a slight brown in color. Toss in onion and garlic and leave for 3 minutes.

2. Add the rice, soup mix and paprika; allow the rice to coat with soup mix and leave for 2 minutes.

3. Add the broth and allow the mixture to boil. Add the tomatoes and allow the mixture to simmer. Cover with lid.

4. Place the dish in the oven and bake for 16 minutes. Add shrimp and peas and cook for 6 more minutes. Transfer from oven and allow to rest for 12 minutes prior to removing the cover. With the use of a fork fluff the rice and adjust seasonings with pepper. Serve warm.

5. Enjoy.

VEGAN
One Pot Dinner

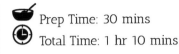

Prep Time: 30 mins
Total Time: 1 hr 10 mins

Servings per Recipe: 8	
Calories	260.1
Fat	6.7g
Cholesterol	0.0mg
Sodium	461.2mg
Carbohydrates	45.5g
Protein	6.6g

Ingredients

1 pinch saffron
1 medium eggplant, cut into chunks
3 tbsp. extra virgin olive oil
1 yellow onion, chopped
5 garlic cloves, crushed
1 yellow pepper, chopped
1 red bell pepper, chopped
1 tsp. dried cilantro
2 tsps. sweet Spanish paprika
1 C. Arborio rice
3 1/2 C. vegetable broth
1 (15 ounce) cans diced tomatoes
1/2 tsp. cayenne powder
1/2 tsp. sea salt
1 tsp. dried thyme
ground black pepper
1 C. mushroom, sliced
1 C. green beans, cut into thirds
1 (15 ounce) cans chickpeas, rinsed and drained
1/4 C. pitted black olives, sliced
1 tbsp. parsley, minced

Directions

1. Pour 3 tbsp of water over saffron in a bowl and leave aside. Sprinkle salt on eggplant pieces and place in a colander for 35 minutes. Rinse the pieces and drain with the use of a colander.

2. Pour olive oil into a skillet and heat well. Toss in the onion, cilantro, garlic, eggplant and peppers and sauté for 6 minutes. Sprinkle paprika and combine the ingredients well. Stir in the rice, tomatoes, saffron water, vegetable stock, cayenne, salt, thyme and ground black pepper. Allow the mixture to boil, lower the heat and allow to simmer. Cook uncovered for 16 minutes. Combine well.

3. Toss in the mushrooms, chickpeas and green beans. Cook without a lid ensuring to stir often and leave for another 16 minutes until the rice becomes tender and the sauce becomes thick in consistency. To keep the rice moist more broth, white wine or water may be added as required.

4. Increase the heat to high for 6 minutes until the bottom forms a caramelized crust. Check the crust with the use of a fork, ensuring not to burn the rice. Remove from heat and allow to sit for 6 minutes. Garnish with olive slices and fresh parsley and serve warm.

5. Enjoy.

30-Minute
Wednesday Paella

🥣 Prep Time: 10 mins
🕐 Total Time: 30mins

Servings per Recipe: 6
Calories	220.3
Fat	9.4g
Cholesterol	101.3mg
Sodium	445.2mg
Carbohydrates	10.9g
Protein	22.6g

Ingredients

3 C. quick-cooking brown rice
1 C. frozen peas
1 tbsp. olive oil
2 chicken breasts, of approx. 4oz each diced
1 medium yellow onion, chopped
2 garlic cloves, minced
4 ounces fully cooked smoked turkey sausage, sliced

1 (15 ounce) cans crushed tomatoes
1/4 tsp. saffron thread
1/4 tsp. turmeric
1/4 tsp. paprika
1/4-1/2 tsp. hot seasoning sauce
8 ounces medium shrimp, peeled and deveined

Directions

1. Cook the brown rice as per package instructions. Transfer the rice from the heat, stir in the peas, cover with lid and allow to stand for 6 minutes.
2. Pour oil into a pan and heat well. Sauté the chicken until cooked; take out from the heat and leave aside.
3. Toss in onion and garlic and leave for 4 minutes until soft.
4. Stir in the sausage into the pan and allow to heat through.
5. Add tomatoes, seasonings and spices and allow the mixture to simmer. Toss in the shrimp, cover with lid and cook for 4 minutes until shrimp is pink in color.
6. Fold in the brown rice and chicken.
7. Enjoy.

CENTRAL
American Paella
(Belizean Inspired)

Prep Time: 45 mins
Total Time: 1 hr 45 mins

Servings per Recipe: 6
Calories   393.2
Fat   11.0g
Cholesterol   26.1mg
Sodium   539.4mg
Carbohydrates   51.9g
Protein   21.5g

Ingredients

1/4 C. olive oil
16 ounces scallops
1 large onion, chopped
2 garlic cloves, minced
1 1/2 C. rice
3 1/4 C. fish stock
1/4 tsp. saffron
salt and pepper
1 red bell pepper, roasted and cut in strips

18 mild green canned chilies
1 (14 ounce) cans artichoke hearts, drained and sprinkled with lemon juice
lemon wedge

Directions

1. Pour half the quantity of olive oil into a skillet and heat well. Toss in the scallops and temper for 4 minutes. Transfer the scallops to a dish and dispose the pan juices.
2. Pour the balance olive oil into the skillet and sauté the onion and garlic for 6 minutes. Stir in the rice and allow to cook for 6 more minutes. Fold in the saffron, broth, salt and pepper and leave to cook for 12 minutes. Stir in the chilies and roasted red bell peppers and allow to cook for another 12 minutes. Fold in the artichoke hearts and fried scallops and allow to cook for 6 minutes until the liquid has been fully absorbed and the rice is soft and tender.
3. Serve garnished with wedges of lemon or additional roasted sweet red bell pepper strips. Serve warm.
4. Enjoy.

Paella
Rustica

Prep Time: 45 mins
Total Time: 1 hr 45 mins

Servings per Recipe: 4
Calories	1504.0
Fat	69.5g
Cholesterol	340.1mg
Sodium	329.8mg
Carbohydrates	115.2g
Protein	96.6g

Ingredients

4 - 8 chicken
2 onions, chopped
1 - 3 garlic clove, chopped
1 tsp. turmeric
115 - 250 g chorizo sausage, cooked
250 g rice
1 liter stock

4 tomatoes, peeled and chopped
1 red pepper
1 C. peas
salt and pepper

Directions

1. Rub paprika on the chicken and place the chicken in a skillet and leave until nicely browned. Transfer the chicken to a side of the skillet.
2. Sauté the onions for a few minutes.
3. Stir in the garlic and turmeric and allow to cook for a few minutes.
4. Toss in the chorizo and stir fry for a few minutes.
5. Fold in rice and half the quantity of stock. If you prefer a spicy paella add balsamic/lee, red wine/sherry and Perrins etc.
6. Stir in the peppers, tomato and vegetables.
7. Place on the hob until the rice is done, add stock as required.
8. Sprinkle parsley, bacon and peppers on top.
9. Serve garnished with white wine and French or Spanish bread.
10. Enjoy.

PAELLA
Trinidad

Prep Time: 10 mins
Total Time: 1 hr 10 mins

Servings per Recipe: 8

Calories	462.6
Fat	17.1g
Cholesterol	121.9mg
Sodium	1008.7mg
Carbohydrates	44.5g
Protein	28.3g

Ingredients

1 lb. large shrimp, peeled and deveined
1 green bell pepper, seeded and sliced into strips
3 chicken breasts, strips
3 smoked sausage, sliced
1 large onion, chopped
1 (14 1/2 ounce) cans diced tomatoes, undrained
2 C. sweet rice
3 C. chicken broth
1/3 C. dry red wine
1/2 tsp. saffron thread
1 piece bay leaf
1/2 tsp. salt
1/2 C. frozen peas, thawed
1/2 C. seafood
2 tbsp. oil

Directions

1. Marinate the shrimps with ¼ tsp salt, 1 tsp minced garlic, ¼ tsp black pepper, 1 tbsp oil and ½ tsp Old Bay seasoning. Use a plastic wrap to cover and leave in the refrigerator.

2. Pour oil into a skillet and sauté the strips of green bell pepper, remove to a bowl and leave aside. Pour additional oil and sauté the chicken breast for 4 minutes per side. Place the cooked chicken towards the sides of the skillet, and stir in chorizos or smoked sausages into the skillet. Allow the chorizos to brown for about 5 minutes. Remove the chicken and chorizo to a platter and leave aside.

3. Pour 2 tbsp of oil into the skillet and stir fry the onions until soft. Toss in the tomatoes along with the juice and 2 C. of rice and combine well until the tomato mixture coats the sweet rice.

4. Pour chicken broth and wine over the ingredients. Add bay leaf, saffron threads and cooked chorizos and chicken and allow the mixture to boil. Stir once in a while.

5. Transfer the mixture to a baking dish, cover with lid and leave in the oven for 22 minutes at a temperature of 350F until the rice is done and the mixture becomes dry. Remove lid and arrange the shrimp, bell peppers and seafood mix. Cover with lid and place back again in the oven and bake for 16 minutes. Take out from the oven and allow the mixture to stand for 6 minutes.

6. Enjoy.

Florentine
Paella

Prep Time: 10 mins
Total Time: 40 mins

Servings per Recipe: 4
Calories	551.8
Fat	14.4g
Cholesterol	0.0mg
Sodium	47.8mg
Carbohydrates	91.1g
Protein	8.6g

Ingredients

3 C. water
1/2 C. white wine
1 1/2 lbs. ripe tomatoes, cored and cut into wedges
salt & ground black pepper
1/4 C. extra virgin olive oil
1 medium onion, minced

1 tbsp. minced garlic
1 tbsp. tomato paste
1 pinch saffron thread
1 - 2 tsp. paprika
2 C. short-grain rice
minced parsley, and basil

Directions

1. Before you do anything set the oven to 450F. Pour water into a pot and heat well. Place the tomatoes in a bowl, sprinkle salt and pepper on top and pour 1 tbsp of olive oil on the tomatoes. Allow to coat well.

2. Pour the balance oil in an ovenproof dish. Sauté onion and garlic and add salt to the pan and cook for 6 minutes until the veggies are soft. Pour tomato paste, paprika and saffron and cook for 2 more minutes. Fold in the rice and cook for 3 minutes. Pour wine and allow to simmer until the mixture is dry, then fold in the warm water and combine well.

3. Arrange wedges of tomato on the rice and drizzle the juices from the bowl on top. Place the ovenproof dish in the oven and leave for 16 minutes. If the rice is still uncooked place the pan once again in the oven and cook for further 12 minutes. If the rice is too dry add more stock or water. Once the rice is cooked switch off the oven and allow the dish to stand for 16 minutes. Take out the pan from oven, sprinkle basil and parsley on top.

4. Enjoy..

PAELLA
Cutlets

Prep Time: 25 mins
Total Time: 55 mins

Servings per Recipe: 1
Calories	108.6
Fat	4.8g
Cholesterol	32.3mg
Sodium	385.2mg
Carbohydrates	9.9g
Protein	5.8g

Ingredients

2 1/2 C. risotto rice
1 large onion, medium chopped
1 bay leaf
2 tsps. crushed garlic
1 chicken bouillon cube
1 1/2 tsps. saffron, crushed
1 tbsp. olive oil
5 C. chicken stock, heated
6 ounces salami
6 ounces smoked ham

seasoned flour
2 eggs, beaten with a little milk
seasoned dry breadcrumb
oil
parsley

Directions

1. Place rice in a saucepan. Add bay leaf, bouillon cube, olive oil, saffron/turmeric and garlic. Stir in hot water/stock into the saucepan. Allow the mixture to boil. Reduce the heat and allow to simmer for about 18 minutes until the liquid is fully absorbed.
2. Take out from the heat; discard the bay leaf and allow the mixture to cool in the room temperature.
3. Place the meats in a food processor, mince and add onto the rice mix. Form balls out of the mixture, if the mixture is too moist fold in bread crumbs or a bit of flour.
4. Roll the balls in seasoned flour until fully covered.
5. Dip them in the egg whip and then roll on breadcrumbs.
6. Leave overnight in the refrigerator.
7. Deep fry the balls in oil at a temperature of 365F until crispy and golden in color.
8. Sprinkle parsley on top and serve.
9. Enjoy.

Paella
Confetti

🥣 Prep Time: 30 mins
🕐 Total Time: 1 hr

Servings per Recipe: 4
Calories   345.4
Fat   19.6g
Cholesterol   97.8mg
Sodium   760.6mg
Carbohydrates   22.0g
Protein   20.3g

Ingredients

1 large cauliflower
2 tbsp. olive oil
1 onion, diced
1 red bell pepper, diced
1 yellow bell pepper, diced
4 garlic cloves, minced
1 tsp. paprika

2 pinches saffron threads
1/2 lemon juice, and zest
1/4 C. dry white wine
2 Spanish chorizo sausages, sliced
1/2 lb. shrimp, deveined
1/4 C. parsley, chopped

Directions

1. Chop the cauliflower into small florets and place in a food processor. Process until it forms the consistency of grain and leave aside.
2. Pour oil into a pan and heat well. Toss in onion and temper until soft. Stir in the garlic and bell pepper and leave until slightly browned. Add the cauliflower, spices, white wine and stock or paella base. Fold in ham and chorizo and leave for about 6 minutes. If chorizo needs further cooking leave for additional 12 minutes.
3. Stir in shrimp and parsley and leave until the shrimp turns pink in color.
4. Serve warm.
5. Enjoy.

BABY
Paella

Prep Time: 20 mins
Total Time: 45 mins

Servings per Recipe: 4
Calories   702.4
Fat   24.8g
Cholesterol   218.0mg
Sodium   1918.2mg
Carbohydrates   70.5g
Protein   45.6g

Ingredients

1 whole chicken breasts, boned
1/4 lb. chicken livers
1/4 lb. lean pork, diced
1/4 C. olive oil
1 garlic clove, minced
1 pimiento, drained and diced
1 tomatoes, peeled and chopped
4 ounces frozen baby lima beans
1 1/2 C. rice
2 3/4 C. broth

1 1/2 tsps. salt
1/4 tsp. saffron
7 - 8 ounces clams
4 1/2 ounces large shrimp

Directions

1. Slice the chicken into 1" chunks. Pour olive oil into a skillet and sauté the pork and chicken livers until a light brown in color.
2. Toss in pimiento, garlic and tomato and cook for 2 minutes. Stir in the defrosted limas and rice and allow to coat evenly with oil.
3. Mix saffron with broth or water, add clams and juice and allow the mixture to boil. Pour the hot liquid over the rice.
4. Allow the mixture to boil and leave for 17 minutes. Toss in shrimp, cover with lid and maintain the warmth or place in a hot oven of 300F.
5. Leave for 12 minutes until the rice is tender and fluffy.
6. Enjoy.

Milanese
Paella

Prep Time: 15 mins
Total Time: 15 mins

Servings per Recipe: 4
Calories	645.2
Fat	17.1g
Cholesterol	105.6mg
Sodium	889.2mg
Carbohydrates	91.3g
Protein	29.7g

Ingredients

4 C. fish stock

2 tsps. sweet smoked paprika

1 pinch salt

1/4-1/2 C. extra virgin olive oil

2 small lobsters, split in half

1 1/2 large brown onions, peeled & diced

1 red bell pepper, seeds & stem removed, chopped

3 garlic cloves, peeled & minced

2 C. Arborio rice

1 dozen small clam, scrubbed

2 fillets, white fish fillets cut into pieces

2 tbsp. parsley, chopped

2 lemons wedges

Directions

1. Place fish broth, salt and pimenton in a saucepan and heat on a low flame. In the meantime, pour the olive oil into a skillet and heat until almost smoking on a barbeque.

2. Toss in the prawns, flip once in a while and allow to cook for 8 minutes until a slight brown in color. Transfer the prawns to a platter and toss in the lobsters to the skillet, with shell side facing downwards and cook for 5 minutes, turn on the other side and leave for further 5 minutes.

3. Remove the lobsters and place in the platter with prawns. If the skillet is too dry, add more oil. Lower the heat to medium, fold in the pepper, onions and garlic and allow to cook for 12 minutes until soft.

4. Fold in the rice into the skillet and mix with the vegetables.

5. Pour the broth into skillet and allow the mixture to boil, then reduce the heat and allow to simmer for 12 minutes.

6. Lay the prawns, clams, lobster and fish on the surface of the rice, cover with aluminum foil and allow to cook for 12 minutes.

7. Take out the foil cover and cook for further 6 minutes. The rice should be cooked through and the clams should open up.

8. Remove from heat, cover once again with the foil and leave for 16 minutes. Sprinkle parsley on top before serving.

9. Enjoy.

GOLDEN
Paella

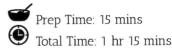

Prep Time: 15 mins
Total Time: 1 hr 15 mins

Servings per Recipe: 6
Calories	1014.5
Fat	61.5g
Cholesterol	310.1mg
Sodium	943.1mg
Carbohydrates	71.4g
Protein	42.4g

Ingredients

Aioli
2 large egg yolks
1 garlic clove, minced
1 pinch saffron thread
kosher salt
1 C. olive oil
3 tbsp. olive oil
1 tsp. lemon juice
Paella
5 tbsp. extra virgin olive oil
2 onions, diced
5 large plum tomatoes, halved
2 red bell peppers, cored and diced
3 bay leaves
1 tsp. paprika
4 C. fish stock
2 C. short-grain rice
1 C. peas
12 ounces squid rings
1 1/2 lbs. mussels
12 ounces large shrimp, peeled with tails intact
2 tbsp. fresh parsley, chopped
lemon wedge

Directions

1. Whisk the egg yolks, saffron, garlic and a dash of salt with the use of a mixer with the whisk attachment; add olive oil drop by drop.
2. Once the aioli becomes thick in consistency increase the flow of oil into a thin stream; add a bit of lemon juice and more salt if required.
3. Pour olive oil into a skillet with lid and heat well; toss in the onion and temper for 16 minutes until soft.
4. In the meantime, grate the plum tomatoes, slice the edges until the skins are left and dispose the skins.
5. Fold in the tomatoes, bay leaves and peppers to the onions; adjust seasonings with paprika.
6. Allow the mixture to simmer, stir once in a while for about 16 minutes.
7. Pour the stock and allow the mixture to boil. Fold in the rice, lower the heat and allow to simmer for 12 minutes preventing the rice getting stuck to the bottom of the skillet.
8. Add the peas, mussels or clams, squid and shrimp; reduce the heat and allow to simmer for 12 minutes until the liquid becomes fully absorbed.
9. Cover the skillet with lid, transfer from heat and allow to rest for 12 minutes; sprinkle parsley on top and allow the mixture to cool.
10. Serve garnished with wedges of lemon and saffron aioli.
11. Enjoy.

Riverside
Paella

🥣 Prep Time: 1 hr

🕐 Total Time: 1 hr 55 mins

Servings per Recipe: 6

Calories	873.9
Fat	38.9g
Cholesterol	83.9mg
Sodium	1021.5mg
Carbohydrates	88.7g
Protein	34.4g

Ingredients

5 C. chicken broth

1/4 tsp. saffron thread

1 1/2 lbs. loin lamb, trimmed fat

1/2 tsp. salt

1/2 tsp. ground black pepper

3 tbsp. olive oil

6 ounces thick-cut pancetta, diced

1 large leek, halved lengthwise then sliced

8 baby artichokes, halved, outer leaves removed, stems trimmed

1 C. dry light white wine

2 tbsp. chopped rosemary

2 1/2 C. Arborio rice

1 1/2 C. shelled peas

Directions

1. Place the saffron and broth in a pot and heat well. Reduce the heat, cover with lid and maintain the warmth.
2. Place the oven rack in the middle of the oven and before you do anything set the oven to 375F. Rub salt and pepper on lamb loin.
3. Pour olive oil into a skillet and sauté the loin for 7 minutes until a slight brown on all sides; remove the loin to a platter and leave aside.
4. Stir in the pancetta to the skillet, stir often and leave for 5 minutes until a slight brown in color.
5. Toss in the leeks and leave for 4 minutes until soft.
6. Add the baby artichoke halves and leave for 2 minutes until fragrant.
7. Stir in the rosemary and wine; allow the mixture to simmer ensuring to scrape up any food pieces stuck to the bottom of the pan.
8. Leave for 6 minutes until the sauce becomes thick in consistency; stir the mixture occasionally.
9. Fold in the rice and leave for 2 minutes allowing the rice to coat evenly with the sauce.
10. Stir in the warm broth mix and allow to simmer.
11. Lower the heat, uncover and allow to simmer for 12 minutes stirring once in a while.
12. Cut the lamb into 1" parts.
13. Once the rice has cooked in 12 minutes, fold in the lamb parts into the bubbling sauce. Sprinkle peas on top.
14. Place in the preheated oven and leave for about 16 minutes until the liquid becomes dry and the rice is soft and tender.
15. Take out from the oven, place on a wire rack, cover with the use of a foil, and leave for 12 minutes to come to room temperature prior to serving.
16. Enjoy.

SOUTHWEST
Paella

Prep Time: 10 mins
Total Time: 55 mins

Servings per Recipe: 6
Calories	576.0
Fat	21.0g
Cholesterol	149.2mg
Sodium	691.5mg
Carbohydrates	58.9g
Protein	39.1g

Ingredients

1/2 lb. frozen shrimp
1/2 lb. frozen clam
1/2 lb. frozen pollock
1/2 lb. frozen octopus
2 tbsp. clarified butter
1 (6 ounce) cans chipotle chilies in adobo
2 tbsp. bouquet garni
2 tbsp. garlic
2 C. saffron rice mix

1 bay leaf
1 large Vidalia onion
6 C. water
1 (12 ounce) cans black beans
6 tortillas, deep fried
2 avocados, wedges
2 limes wedges

Directions

1. Place the clarified butter in a saucepan and allow to melt.
2. Sauté the onions and leave until nearly caramelized.
3. Toss in bouquet garni and bay leaf.
4. Pour water over the ingredients and combine well.
5. Stir in the seafood mix and allow the mixture to boil for 8 minutes.
6. Lower the heat and allow the mixture to simmer. Toss in garlic chipotles in Adobo, garlic or sundried tomato mixture, cover with lid and cook for 48 minutes.
7. Take away the bay leaf and serve into bowls. Serve garnished with lime and avocado.
8. Enjoy.

Paella
Calamari

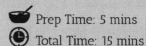 Prep Time: 5 mins
Total Time: 15 mins

Servings per Recipe: 2
Calories	891.2
Fat	36.4g
Cholesterol	93.3mg
Sodium	606.0mg
Carbohydrates	88.3g
Protein	41.2g

Ingredients

1/4 C. olive oil
1 C. uncooked rice
1 C. chicken broth
2 ounces white wine
salt
4 shrimp, deveined
4 scallops
4 clams, scrubbed
4 mussels, scrubbed

2 small lobster tails
1 chicken breast, cubed
parsley
1 tsp. garlic
1/2 C. cooked peas
4 pieces calamari

Directions

1. Prepare the rice according to the package instructions. Once the rice is cooked combine with the peas.
2. Pour oil into a skillet and heat well. Temper the garlic and fold in chicken. Leave for a few minutes and stir in the shellfish.
3. Combine the ingredients with wine, salt and pepper.
4. Serve with cooked rice and sprinkle parsley on top.
5. Enjoy.

HONEY
Saffron Paella

Prep Time: 20 mins
Total Time: 30 mins

Servings per Recipe: 6

Calories	529.9
Fat	30.2g
Cholesterol	66.5mg
Sodium	1459.3mg
Carbohydrates	37.7g
Protein	25.0g

Ingredients

1 lb. chorizo sausage, removed from casings
1/2 C. onion, diced
2 garlic cloves, chopped
1 C. pumpkin, cooked
1/2 C. frozen peas
1/2 tsp. cinnamon
1/2 tsp. ground nutmeg
1/8 tsp. ground cloves
parsley

snipped chives
Rice
2 medium tomatoes, chopped
1 tbsp. honey
drizzle olive oil
salt and pepper
4 C. chicken broth
1 pinch saffron thread
1 C. Arborio rice

Directions

1. Before you do anything set the oven to 325F. To roast the tomatoes, combine the tomatoes, olive oil, honey, salt and pepper. Place the mixture on a slightly buttered parchment sheet. Leave in the oven for 22 minutes.

2. Pour the chicken broth into a saucepan and allow the mixture to boil. Stir in Arborio rice and saffron. Reduce the heat and allow the mixture to simmer for about 22 minutes. Ensure not to drain the rice prior to adding to the paella.

3. Place onion, sausage and garlic in a non-stick pan and heat well. Break the sausage into lumps with the use of a wooden spatula.

4. Allow the mixture to brown and fold in the saffron rice, pumpkin, roasted tomatoes, spices and peas.

5. Allow the mixture to simmer for 12 minutes until thick in consistency. Garnish with chives and fresh parsley and serve warm. Enjoy.

Sweet
Mexicana Paella

Prep Time: 20 mins
Total Time: 55 mins

Servings per Recipe: 4
Calories	306.0
Fat	4.5g
Cholesterol	0.0mg
Sodium	165.9mg
Carbohydrates	61.8g
Protein	7.0g

Ingredients

1 tbsp. vegetable oil
1 onion, chopped
2 garlic cloves, minced
1 C. short-grain rice
1/4 tsp. turmeric
2 C. vegetable stock, warm
1/4 tsp. salt
1/4 tsp. pepper
1 sweet red pepper

1 sweet green pepper
2 plum tomatoes
1 1/2 C. corn kernels
1 bunch parsley, chopped, leaves only

Directions

1. Pour oil into a pan and heat well; sauté the onion, rice, garlic and turmeric for 5 minutes until the onion becomes soft.
2. Add stock, salt and pepper; allow the mixture to boil; lower the heat, cover with lid and allow to simmer for 12 minutes.
3. In the meantime, slice peppers in half along the length; take out membranes and core; slice in half crosswise and slice into strips.
4. Core and dice the tomatoes.
5. Add the tomatoes and peppers into the pan; cover and cook for 16 minutes until the rice becomes tender.
6. Fold in the corn; cover with lid and cook for 6 minutes until the liquid becomes fully absorbed.
7. Sprinkle parsley on top.
8. Can be served with a crunchy crisp marinated salad and crusty roll.
9. Enjoy.

ROASTED
Paella

Prep Time: 1 hr
Total Time: 1 hr 50 mins

Servings per Recipe: 8	
Calories	549.7
Fat	15.3g
Cholesterol	137.6mg
Sodium	1011.7mg
Carbohydrates	59.4g
Protein	40.3g

Ingredients

3 tbsp. olive oil
2 medium onions, chopped
1 red bell pepper, seeded and diced
1/4 lb. Spanish chorizo, sliced and diced
2 garlic cloves, minced
1 tbsp. tomato paste
1 1/4 tsps. smoked paprika
salt
ground black pepper
1 lb. medium grain rice
1 C. clam juice
6 C. fish stock
1 tsp. saffron thread
1 lb. mussels, well-scrubbed
1 lb. jumbo shrimp, peeled and deveined
1 lb. cooked chicken, sliced
1 1/2 C. frozen baby peas
2 tbsp. chopped parsley

Directions

1. Before you do anything set the oven to 350F.
2. Pour the olive oil into a skillet and heat well.
3. Add the onions and sauté for 8 minutes until soft.
4. Toss in the bell pepper and leave for 3 minutes until soft.
5. Stir in the chorizo and sauté for 3 minutes until the sausage is evenly coated with the oil.
6. Fold in the garlic and cook for 35 seconds.
7. Stir in the paprika and tomato paste and leave for about 2 minutes until the mixture slightly darkens in color.
8. Adjust seasonings with salt and pepper.
9. Fold in the rice and cook for 2 minutes. Ensure to stir the rice without browning.
10. Pour in the 1 C. of broth and clam juice into the skillet. Move the skillet using pot holders to ensure that the ingredients are evenly spread out and combined together.
11. Allow to cook for 6 minutes until the liquid is fully absorbed.
12. Stir in the balance broth and the saffron and allow the mixture to boil.
13. Cover with lid and place in the oven.
14. Bake for 38 minutes until the liquid evaporates fully.
15. Transfer the skillet from the oven and fold in the shellfish, peas and sausage and combine well.
16. Cover and place once again in the oven and cook for 16 minutes until the shrimp becomes pink and mussels open up.
17. Take out from the oven and serve.
18. Enjoy.

Chicken
and Chorizo Paella

Prep Time: 20 mins
Total Time: 1 hr 20 mins

Servings per Recipe: 8

Calories	275.6
Fat	14.3g
Cholesterol	95.9mg
Sodium	909.7mg
Carbohydrates	8.9g
Protein	26.6g

Ingredients

1 tbsp. olive oil
1/2 lb. boneless skinless chicken breast, cubed
1/2 lb. chorizo sausage, sliced
1 large onion, chopped
1 garlic clove, chopped
1 (10 ounce) packages saffron rice mix (yellow rice)
3 C. water

1 (14 1/2 ounce) cans diced tomatoes
1/2 lb. raw shrimp, peeled and deveined
1 lb. clam, with shells
1 C. frozen peas

Directions

1. Pour the olive oil into a pan and heat well.
2. Toss in the chicken pieces and sauté until a slight brown in color.
3. Take out the chicken from the pan and leave aside.
4. Lower the heat and fold in the slices of sausage and stir fry until nicely browned.
5. Stir in the onion and garlic and leave to cook for 6 minutes until soft; fold in the rice mix, tomatoes and water.
6. Allow the mixture to boil, uncover and leave to simmer for about 22 minutes until the rice becomes tender and the liquid is fully absorbed.
7. Fold in the shrimp, chicken and clams and leave for 12 minutes until the clams open up.
8. Sprinkle peas on top and serve.
9. Enjoy.

PAELLA
Estrellita

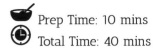

Prep Time: 10 mins
Total Time: 40 mins

Servings per Recipe: 4
Calories	324.8
Fat	7.3g
Cholesterol	40.3mg
Sodium	440.2mg
Carbohydrates	47.2g
Protein	15.9g

Ingredients

1 lb. chorizo sausage, removed from casings
1/2 C. onion, diced
2 garlic cloves, chopped
1 C. pumpkin, cooked
1/2 C. frozen peas
1/2 tsp. cinnamon
1/2 tsp. ground nutmeg
1/8 tsp. ground cloves
parsley

snipped chives
Rice
2 medium tomatoes, chopped
1 tbsp. honey
drizzle olive oil
salt and pepper
4 C. chicken broth
1 pinch saffron thread
1 C. Arborio rice

Directions

1. Add the saffron to the broth and allow the mixture to boil. Add tomato, turmeric, paprika, salt and pepper. Heat oil in a skillet.
2. Sauté onion and garlic until tender, then remove from the skillet.
3. Fold in the chicken and allow to brown, and add oil as necessary, then remove from the skillet. Scrape the bottom of the skillet, pour in more oil, fold in rice and cook until tender.
4. Pour the boiling broth and without stirring cook on a medium flame for 6 minutes.
5. Lower the heat, spread the chicken, mussels, red pepper, chorizo and any other optional ingredients and cook for 16 minutes.
6. Cover with lid and cook on a low heat for 6 more minutes. Move the skillet around to keep the heat even.
7. Allow to stand for 6 minutes, ensuring to dispose shellfish that do not open up.
8. Enjoy.

Paella Winters

Prep Time: 20 mins
Total Time: 3 hr 20 mins

Servings per Recipe: 10
Calories	1117.2
Fat	47.5g
Cholesterol	202.8mg
Sodium	879.9mg
Carbohydrates	116.7g
Protein	58.0g

Ingredients

1 C. olive oil
2 - 3 heads garlic
6 red peppers, cored, seeded and sliced
5 - 6 lbs. chicken
4 yellow onions, chopped
2 (16 ounce) cans diced tomatoes
6 - 7 1/2 C. chicken stock
20 - 25 saffron threads, crushed
2 - 2 1/2 tsps. smoked paprika

4 - 5 C. short-grain rice
2 (16 ounce) cans garbanzo beans
1 lb. green beans
20 - 24 jumbo shrimp
20 - 24 clams
4 - 5 lemons wedges

Directions

1. Pour olive oil into a skillet and heat well. Sauté garlic and peppers in the heated oil. Transfer the peppers from the skillet to a dish and leave aside. Toss in the chicken and leave to sear on all sides until golden brown in color. Stir in the onions and cook until soft.

2. Fold in the tomatoes and the stock and leave for 30 minutes.

3. In the meantime, use a mortar and pestle and pound the smoked paprika and saffron and mix it with the stock.

4. After completion of 30 minutes add the rice and allow to simmer for 22 minutes.

5. Ensure not to cover or stir the rice; when the rice is being cooked toss in the garbanzo beans and the vegetables.

6. Add the shellfish and the shrimp into the rice during the last 10 minutes. Finally add the wedges of lemon onto the rim of the skillet.

7. Serve warm. Enjoy.

PAELLA
Summers

Prep Time: 20 mins
Total Time: 1 hr 20 mins

Servings per Recipe: 6

Calories	750.7
Fat	32.5g
Cholesterol	126.8mg
Sodium	976.6mg
Carbohydrates	73.9g
Protein	38.0g

Ingredients

11 ounces raw shrimp, shells on
2 1/4 lbs. mussels
3/4 C. olive oil
1 small onion, chopped
1 garlic clove, chopped
1 large tomatoes, chopped
2 small squid, cleaned and cut into rings
1 lb. long-grain rice
sea salt
3 sprigs fresh parsley

1 pinch saffron thread
2 chicken stock cubes
4 ounces frozen peas
1 red pepper, deseeded and cut into strips
lemon, wedges

Directions

1. Remove the skin and the tails from the shrimp and leave aside. Place the shells and heads in a saucepan of water and allow to simmer for 12 minutes. Transfer from heat and with the use of a colander strain the liquid into a dish.
2. Take out the beards from the mussels and rinse under tap of running water.
3. Dispose shellfish with damaged shells or which don't close when properly tapped.
4. Place the shellfish in a skillet, stir in 1/4 C. of water, cover with lid and cook for 7 minutes until the shells open up.
5. Remove with a spatula and dispose any shellfish that remain closed up. Keep aside the cooking liquid.
6. Remove the shells from the mussels, keeping aside a few shells for garnishing. Add the cooking liquid to the shrimp stock.
7. 7 C. are required and add water as necessary. Fold in the stock into a pot and heat well without boiling.

8. Set the oven to 350F and pour oil into the skillet.
9. Toss in the onion and garlic and cook for 8 minutes until a slight brown in color.
10. Stir in the tomato and leave for a few minutes.
11. Keep a side a little shrimp for garnishing and stir in the balance to the skillet with rice.
12. Allow to cook until the squid is no longer pink. Stir in the mussels and adjust seasonings with salt and add the stock.
13. Toss the skillet gently ensuring to distribute the liquid evenly.
14. Batch the parsley and saffron together; add 2 tbsp water and stir into the skillet. Break the stock cubes into the skillet and combine well.
15. Stir in the peas and leave for a few minutes.
16. Serve garnished with red pepper, kept aside mussels and shrimps. Place in the oven and cook for 30 minutes.
17. Decorate the rim of the skillet with wedges of lemon.
18. Enjoy.

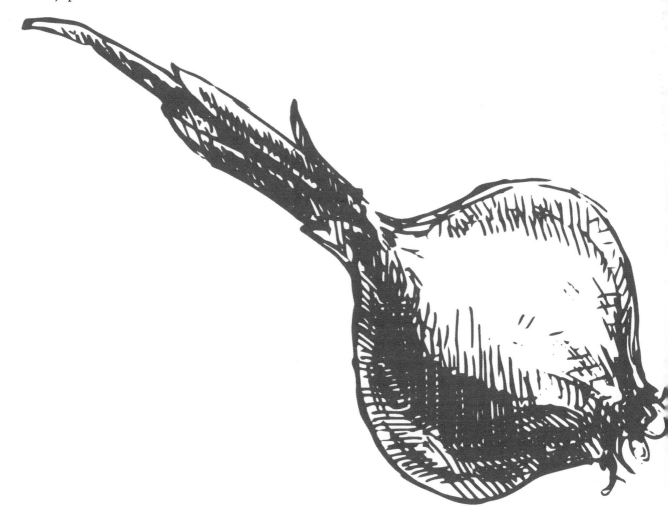

WHITE
and Brown Rice Paella

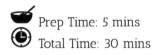 Prep Time: 5 mins
Total Time: 30 mins

Servings per Recipe: 2
Calories	784.3
Fat	40.6g
Cholesterol	119.0mg
Sodium	819.0mg
Carbohydrates	70.1g
Protein	35.8g

Ingredients

1/4 C. long grain white rice
1/4 C. long grain brown rice
1/2 C. coconut milk
1/4 C. water
3 tbsp. crushed pineapple
8 andouille sausages, slices
1/4 lb. chorizo sausage

8 white pearl onions
1/4 lb. catfish, cut into pieces
8 large shrimp

Directions

1. Pour coconut milk and water into a pan and add rice. Allow the mixture to boil, lower the heat and allow to simmer for 12 minutes.
2. Stir in the balance ingredients excluding shrimp and cook for further 12 minutes; stir often.
3. At this point the rice should be half cooked and there should be some liquid left in the pan. Add more water if required.
4. Toss in the shrimp and allow to cook until they are pink in color.
5. If the mixture is moist, take out the shrimp and continue to cook until the liquid is fully absorbed. Add the shrimp once again and serve.
6. Enjoy..

Portuguese Pan

Prep Time: 45 mins
Total Time: 1 hr 40 mins

Servings per Recipe: 6
Calories	465.5
Fat	19.7g
Cholesterol	219.1mg
Sodium	1142.8mg
Carbohydrates	38.5g
Protein	31.7g

Ingredients

1/2 lb. chorizo sausage
1 small red bell pepper, chopped
1 small yellow bell pepper, chopped
1 onion, chopped
2 garlic cloves, minced
1/4 tsp. crushed saffron thread
1 lb. shrimp, peeled, deveined, and chopped
1 (3 1/2 ounce) cans smoked mussels, drained
2 C. cooked white rice

1 C. Italian seasoned breadcrumbs
1/2 C. chopped flat leaf parsley
1/4 C. green olives, sliced
2 tbsp. lemon juice
1/2 tsp. ground cumin
1/2 tsp. cayenne pepper
1/4 tsp. salt
2 eggs

Directions

1. Before you do anything set the oven to 350F; remove the sausage from its cover and break the meat into a non-stick pan.
2. Cook the sausage, stir once in a while and allow to cook for 6 minutes until a slight brown in color.
3. Drain the excess grease; stir in the onions and peppers into the pan.
4. Lower the heat, stir once in a while and leave for 6 minutes until the vegetables are soft.
5. Fold in the saffron and garlic, stir and allow to cook for 2 minutes.
6. Place the shrimp, rice, mussels, parsley, bread crumbs, lemon juice, olive, cayenne, cumin, eggs, salt and cooked vegetable/sausage mixture in a bowl and combine well with the use of your hands.
7. Fold in the mixture to a loaf pan; bake for 50 minutes until the top is crusty and the loaf becomes brown in color.
8. Allow the loaf to stand in the loaf pan for 12 minutes. Slice into squares and serve.
9. Enjoy.

OUR
Best Paella

🥣 Prep Time: 25 mins

🕐 Total Time: 1 hr 25 mins

Servings per Recipe: 10	
Calories	347.3
Fat	9.0g
Cholesterol	151.4mg
Sodium	1257.6mg
Carbohydrates	38.4g
Protein	26.4g

Ingredients

8 ounces sausage, cut into pieces
15 raw chicken strips
2 lbs. large shrimp
1 onion, chopped
1 green bell pepper
1 stalk celery, chopped
2 garlic cloves, minced
2 C. uncooked long grain rice

2 (14 1/2 ounce) cans diced tomatoes
2 bay leaves
2 tsps. salt
1 tsp. dried oregano
3/4 tsp. ground turmeric
3 1/2 C. chicken broth

Directions

1. Heat a skillet and sauté sausage pieces until nicely browned on all sides. Transfer the sausage into a platter, and sauté the chicken in the sausage fat until nicely browned.

2. Transfer the chicken into the platter. Stir fry the onions, celery, green pepper and garlic for 6 minutes until soft.

3. Fold in the rice, bay leaves, tomatoes, turmeric, oregano and salt, combine well and cook for 2 minutes. Fold in the chicken broth and the kept aside tomato juice into the mixture.

4. Stir in the chicken, cover with lid and allow to simmer for 22 minutes.

5. Toss in the sausages and allow to simmer for 16 minutes; add the shrimp, cover with lid and cook for 12 minutes until the shrimp becomes pink in color.

6. Enjoy.

Paella
Zaragoza

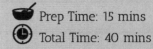

Prep Time: 15 mins
Total Time: 40 mins

Servings per Recipe: 8
Calories   629.4
Fat   26.0g
Cholesterol   173.6mg
Sodium   1447.3mg
Carbohydrates   47.7g
Protein   47.5g

Ingredients

3 tbsp. extra virgin olive oil
3 garlic cloves, crushed
1/2 tsp. crushed red pepper flakes
2 C. enriched white rice
1/4 tsp. saffron thread
1 bay leaf
1 quart chicken broth
4 spring thyme
1 1/2 lbs. chicken tenders, cut into thirds
salt
ground pepper
1 red bell pepper, seeded and chopped
Toppings
1 medium onion, chopped
3/4 lb. chorizo sausage, casing removed and sliced
1 lb. large shrimp, peeled and deveined
18 green lipped mussels, cleaned
1 C. frozen peas
2 lemons, zested
1/4 C. flat leaf parsley, chopped
4 scallions, chopped
lemon wedge
crusty bread

Directions

1. Pour 2 tbsp extra virgin olive oil into a skillet and heat well. Add the garlic, rice and red pepper flakes and sauté for 4 minutes

2. Fold in saffron threads, broth, bay leaf and thyme and allow the mixture to boil. Cover with lid and allow the mixture to simmer.

3. Add 1 tbsp of extra virgin olive oil into another skillet and brown the chicken on all sides. Sprinkle salt and pepper on the chicken.

4. Toss in onions and peppers to the skillet and leave for 4 minutes. Fold in the chorizo to the skillet and cook for further 3 minutes. Take out the skillet from heat.

5. After about 15 minutes, stir in the shellfish to the rice. Sprinkle peas and lemon zest over the rice mixture, then cover with lid. After 6 minutes remove the lid and dispose any mussel shells which do not open up.

6. Fold in the rice and seafood mix and discard the bay and thyme leaves. Spread the chicken, onions, peppers and chorizo in the skillet.

7. Sprinkle parsley and scallions on top.

8. Serve garnished with lemon wedges and warm crusty bread.

9. Enjoy.

POLISH
Paella

Prep Time: 20 mins
Total Time: 45 mins

Servings per Recipe: 6
Calories   635.0
Fat   26.8g
Cholesterol   101.9mg
Sodium   960.0mg
Carbohydrates   61.3g
Protein   34.0g

Ingredients

1 lb. boneless skinless chicken, cubed
1 lb. kielbasa, cubed
1 medium onion, diced
1 tbsp. bottled garlic
1 tomatoes, diced
1 bell pepper, diced
1/2 C. frozen peas
3 C. chicken stock

2 C. long-grain rice
1 tbsp. olive oil
1 tsp. turmeric
1 bay leaf
salt & pepper

Directions

1. Before you do anything set the oven to 350F.
2. Rub salt and pepper on the chicken.
3. Pour oil into a pan with lid and heat well; pan fry the chicken until a nice brown in color.
4. Transfer the chicken from the pan.
5. Place the pan once again on the heat and fold in onion, kielbasa and bell pepper.
6. Pan fry until the kielbasa turns brown and the onions become soft.
7. Fold in the tomato and transfer the chicken back again into the pan.
8. Add the rice, chicken stock, bay leaf and the turmeric.
9. Allow the mixture to boil.
10. Place the peas on top.
11. Cover the pan with lid and set in the oven.
12. Bake for 27 minutes until the rice is cooked and the liquid is absorbed.
13. Enjoy.

City
Park Paella

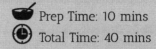 Prep Time: 10 mins

Total Time: 40 mins

Servings per Recipe: 4

Calories	559.0
Fat	18.9g
Cholesterol	161.5mg
Sodium	1166.4mg
Carbohydrates	62.0g
Protein	37.4g

Ingredients

1 tbsp. olive oil
1/2 C. onion, chopped
6 ounces chicken sausage, cooked and sliced
2 (3 1/2 ounce) packages brown rice
salt
1/2 tsp. smoked paprika
1/4 tsp. black pepper

1 (15 ounce) cans chicken broth
1 (14 1/2 ounce) cans diced tomatoes, undrained
2 tsps. garlic, minced
1 1/2 C. edamame, frozen. shelled
1/4 tsp. saffron thread
1/2 lb. frozen shrimp, thawed

Directions

1. Pour oil into a skillet and heat well. Toss in onions and sausage and pan fry until the onions become soft.
2. Fold in the rice to the skillet.
3. Stir frequently and add the paprika, salt and pepper and fry for 32 seconds.
4. Fold in tomatoes, chicken broth and garlic and allow the mixture to boil.
5. Cover with lid and allow to simmer for 12 minutes until the liquid is fully absorbed and rice is cooked.
6. Add the saffron and edamame.
7. Fold in the shrimp to the rice mix, cover with lid and cook for 5 minutes until the liquid is fully absorbed.
8. Enjoy.

NEW ENGLAND
Paella

Prep Time: 20 mins
Total Time: 1 hr 35 mins

Servings per Recipe: 4
Calories	598.9
Fat	15.1g
Cholesterol	87.2mg
Sodium	832.8mg
Carbohydrates	75.8g
Protein	27.7g

Ingredients

4 lobster tails
8 stone crab claws
12 large shrimp
8 large clams, washed and scrubbed
8 large mussels, washed and scrubbed
2 green peppers, seeded and chopped
4 -5 plum tomatoes, peeled and
chopped
2 cloves garlic, peeled and minced
1/8 tsp. red pepper flakes
salt and pepper
1 pinch saffron
1 1/2 C. long grain rice, rinsed
1/4 C. unsalted butter, softened
3 C. chicken broth
1 C. dry white wine
1 (10 ounce) boxes frozen green peas
roasted red pepper, strips

Directions

1. Before you do anything set the oven to 400F.
2. Pour salted water into a saucepan and heat mussels, clams and shrimp and leave for 4 minutes; transfer from water and leave aside.
3. Throw away any clams or mussels which do not open up.
4. Baste butter on lobster tails.
5. Cover crab claws and lobster tails with aluminum foil and leave in the oven for 16 minutes.
6. Sauté onions, green peppers, garlic and tomatoes in a skillet until garlic become soft.
7. Stir in red pepper flakes, saffron, salt and pepper.
8. Fold in the rice and pan fry for 4 minutes.
9. Add the wine and the broth and allow the mixture to simmer for 22 minutes.
10. Toss in the peas.
11. Cover with lid and allow to cook for 16 minutes.
12. Stir once in a while to ensure the liquid is fully absorbed by the rice.
13. Lay the lobster, shrimp, clams, stone crab and mussels on top.
14. Cover with lid and heat for further 12 minutes.
15. Transfer the mixture to a dish.
16. Serve garnished with roasted red peppers.
17. Enjoy.

Sun
Dried Parmesan Paella

🥣 Prep Time: 20 mins
🕐 Total Time: 50 mins

Servings per Recipe: 6
Calories	443.2
Fat	14.6g
Cholesterol	73.6mg
Sodium	561.8mg
Carbohydrates	43.3g
Protein	32.1g

Ingredients

1 tbsp. oil
1 1/2 C. rice
3 C. chicken broth, rich
1 tsp. turmeric
1/2 tsp. cumin, ground
salt and pepper
1 garlic clove, minced
4 shallots, minced

3 sun-dried tomatoes, drained and chopped
1/4 C. chicken broth
4 C. cooked chicken, diced
1/4 C. pine nuts, toasted
1/4 C. parmesan cheese

Directions

1. Place the first six ingredients in a skillet and leave for 32 minutes until the liquid is fully absorbed and the rice becomes tender.
2. In the meantime, place the next four ingredients in a saucepan and allow to cook until the shallots are tender.
3. Fold in the chicken and allow to heat through.
4. Fold in the tomato mixture into the rice and combine well.
5. Place the mixture in a platter and sprinkle pine nuts and cheese on top.
6. Enjoy.

SOUTHERN
Barcelona Paella

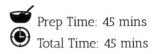 Prep Time: 45 mins
Total Time: 45 mins

Servings per Recipe: 6
Calories   869.1
Fat   36.9g
Cholesterol   121.6mg
Sodium   1320.6mg
Carbohydrates   82.8g
Protein   47.6g

Ingredients

10 medium chicken drumsticks
1/2 C. extra virgin olive oil
2 C. medium shrimp
1 medium Spanish onion, diced
1/2 C. pureed ripe tomatoes
1 tsp. kosher salt
1 tsp. saffron thread
2 tbsp. sweet pimientos
4 quarts chicken stock
2 C. bomba
1 lb. manila clams, scrubbed
1 C. fresh peas
10 asparagus spears, sliced
1 inch piece sausage

Directions

1. Before you do anything set the oven to 400F. Spread the chicken drumsticks on a parchment sheet and season with olive oil and salt. Leave in the oven for 25 minutes and leave aside.

2. Meanwhile, heat a skillet, pour the oil and leave until smoking. Toss in the shrimp and allow to cook until brown in color on all sides, on 4 minutes on each side.

3. Remove to a dish and leave aside. Toss in the onion and cook for 9 minutes until soft. Move the onions into the middle of the pan and add 2 tbsp of salt to the sides of the pan.

4. Stir in the tomato puree and cook for 4 minutes. Sprinkle the balance salt, pimenton and saffron and cook for 6 minutes.

5. Pour chicken stock and allow the mixture to boil for 6 minutes. Fold in the rice and combine well. Stir in clams and drumsticks and arrange them in the pan.

6. Fold in the asparagus and peas and allow the mixture to boil ensuring not to stir, for 12 minutes. Adjust seasonings as required and allow to cook for further 10 minutes until the liquid has evaporated.

7. Transfer from the heat and allow to rest for 12 minutes prior to serving.

8. Enjoy.

Weekend
Paella

Prep Time: 30 mins

Total Time: 2 hrs

Servings per Recipe: 6
Calories	271.4
Fat	9.6g
Cholesterol	8.8mg
Sodium	306.3mg
Carbohydrates	36.9g
Protein	8.6g

Ingredients

2 tbsp. vegetable oil
1 onion, sliced
1 red pepper, cored, seeded and sliced
1 garlic clove, crushed
1 C. long grain rice
1 quart chicken stock
1 tsp. paprika
1 tsp. turmeric

1 C. frozen peas
3/4 C. smoked ham, ends diced
1/4 C. bacon, ends diced

Directions

1. Pour oil into a skillet and heat well. Sauté the onion for 5 minutes until soft. Fold in the bacon and cook until a slight golden in color.
2. Stir in the red pepper, rice and garlic and pan fry for 2 minutes.
3. Fold in the ham, paprika, stock and turmeric and allow the mixture to boil and then simmer for 15 minutes.
4. Combine the mixture with peas and bacon bits and cook for 5 more minutes until the rice and vegetables are soft and tender.
5. Adjust seasonings and serve warm.
6. Enjoy.

PAELLA
Pacifica

Prep Time: 20 mins
Total Time: 40 mins

Servings per Recipe: 2
Calories	301.2
Fat	10.1g
Cholesterol	99.3mg
Sodium	1388.8mg
Carbohydrates	17.6g
Protein	34.7g

Ingredients

12 large shrimp, peeled and deveined
achiote paste
1 tbsp. olive oil
4 tbsp. onions, small dice
1/2 C. chicken stock
1 lb. yellow tomatoes, chopped
1 tsp. yellow bell pepper, chopped
24 clams, washed

8 large basil leaves, torn
cilantro leaf, torn
salt

Directions

1. Combine shrimp and achiote paste and allow to marinate for 22 minutes.
2. Pour oil into a skillet, heat well and sauté the onions until soft.
3. Pour the chicken stock, cover with lid and allow the mixture to boil.
4. Fold in pepper and tomatoes; stir in clams, cover with lid and leave until they pop open for about 8 minutes.
5. Add the shrimp, cover with lid and allow to cook.
6. Season with salt if required; serve garnished with cilantro and basil.
7. Enjoy.

Spanish
Game Paella

Prep Time: 1 hr 15 mins
Total Time: 1 hr 40 mins

Servings per Recipe: 6
Calories   773.3
Fat   35.7g
Cholesterol   75.1mg
Sodium   1434.6mg
Carbohydrates   76.4g
Protein   27.6g

Ingredients

6 tbsp. olive oil
3 quail, quartered
1/2 lb. chorizo sausage, cut into pieces
1 small rabbit, quartered
1 quart beef broth
beef broth
1 C. red wine
1/4 tsp. saffron thread
2 duck confit, legs
1 large yellow onion, chopped

6 garlic cloves, chopped
1 3/4 C. canned diced tomatoes
2 tsps. stemmed thyme
1 1/2 tsps. smoked paprika
1 tsp. salt
1 bay leaf
2 1/2 C. Arborio rice

Directions

1. Pour 2 tbsp olive oil into a pan and heat well.
2. Toss in the quails and brown on all sides for about 10 minutes; remove to a plate.
3. Stir in chorizo and cook for 9 minutes until nicely browned; remove to plate; cover with wrap and leave in the refrigerator.
4. Leave 2 tbsps. fat in the pan and drain the rest; toss in rabbit pieces.
5. Flip once and allow to cook for 9 minutes.
6. Add the broth, saffron and red wine and allow the mixture to simmer, scrape off any food pieces stuck to the bottom of the pan.
7. Cover with lid, reduce heat, and allow to simmer for 32 minutes until the rabbit is soft and tender.
8. Transfer the rabbit into the plate and allow to rest for 12 minutes.
9. Maintain the warmth of the cooking liquid in the pan and there should be about 4 C. of broth.

10. Once the rabbit pieces are cool, remove the meat from the bones, discard the bones and cut the meat into tiny pieces.
11. Remove the meat from the duck confit legs; shred with a fork; leave the meat to cool at room temperature.
12. Place the rack in the middle of the oven and before you do anything set the oven to 375F.
13. Heat a skillet; add the balance 4 tbsp oil and sauté the onion for 5 minutes until soft.
14. Toss in garlic and cook for 2 minutes.
15. Fold in tomatoes, smoked paprika, thyme, bay leaf and salt and leave for 12 minutes until the liquid has evaporated.
16. Fold in the rice to the pan and heat for 2 minutes until soft.
17. Use a colander to strain the hot broth mixture into the pan and allow to cook uncovered for 12 minutes.
18. Fold in the meat into the sauce, spreading it around the pan.
19. Leave in the oven for 16 minutes until the rice is tender and the liquid is fully absorbed.
20. Place on a wire rack, use a foil to cover and leave at room temperature for 12 minutes prior to serving.
21. Enjoy.

Paella Cubano

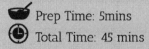

Prep Time: 5mins
Total Time: 45 mins

Servings per Recipe: 4
Calories	1137.7
Fat	50.5g
Cholesterol	145.8mg
Sodium	2817.8mg
Carbohydrates	98.8g
Protein	67.9g

Ingredients

3 tbsp. olive oil
1 lb. smoked sausage, quartered and diced
4 boneless skinless chicken breasts
1 onion, diced small
2 bell peppers, steamed, seeded, diced
1 jalapeno, steamed and seeded, minced
1 tbsp. paprika
1 tbsp. cumin
1/4 tsp. cayenne
4 garlic cloves, minced
1 (14 ounce) cans diced tomatoes, drained and diced
2 C. white rice, rinsed and drained dry
4 C. chicken broth
1 bay leaf
2 tbsp. dried parsley
1 C. frozen peas
salt and pepper

Directions

1. Pour oil into a pan with high edges. Toss in the smoked sausage and allow to brown well. Transfer from the pan and leave aside.

2. Pat dry the chicken breasts and rub salt and pepper on all sides. Brown the chicken breasts in the pan on all sides.

3. Take out from the pan and cover with foil.

4. Toss in the onion and all the variety of peppers and cook, scrape the brown bits from the bottom of the pan. Leave until the vegetables are soft and tender.

5. Toss in the garlic, paprika, cumin and cayenne and cook until aromatic for about 2 minutes. Stir in the rice and tomatoes and combine well.

6. Fold in the chicken broth and stir in the bay leaf. Allow the mixture to boil, cover with lid, lower the heat and allow to simmer.

7. Cook for 32 minutes until the rice is cooked and tender.

8. When the rice is done, adjust seasonings with salt and pepper. Slice the chicken into 1" cubes and add it with the smoked sausage into the pan.

9. Fold in the peas and parsley, cover with lid and cook on a reduced heat and leave until the sausage and chicken is warmed through.

10. Enjoy.

SEATTLE
Vegetarian Paella

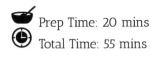

Prep Time: 20 mins
Total Time: 55 mins

Servings per Recipe: 6
Calories	269.6
Fat	6.5g
Cholesterol	0.0mg
Sodium	260.0mg
Carbohydrates	42.1g
Protein	9.0g

Ingredients

1 pinch saffron thread
2 C. vegetable broth
1/2 C. water
4 vegetarian sausages
1 tbsp. olive oil
1 large onion, chopped
salt and pepper
1/4 C. chopped pimiento
1 C. frozen peas
1/3 C. dry sherry
3 tbsp. vegan margarine
1/2 C. orzo pasta
1 C. brown rice
1/2 C. flat leaf parsley, chopped

Directions

1. Pour 1/2 C. of water and 2 C. stock to a saucepan and add the saffron. Allow the mixture to boil, lower the heat and allow to simmer for a few minutes.
2. Place a pan with lid on heat and allow to heat well. Cut the sausages on an angle into 1" thickness. Pour olive oil into the hot pan and toss in the sausages.
3. Allow to cook and brown on all sides for 4 minutes. Leave aside.
4. Pour more oil to the pan and add the onions. Adjust seasonings with salt and pepper and allow to cook for about 4 minutes. Stir in the peas and pimientos.
5. Use sherry to deglaze the pan and stir for 3 minutes. Leave aside.
6. Place the pan once again on heat, add 2 tbsp of butter and allow to melt. Stir in the pasta and leave for 5 minutes until a golden brown in color.
7. Toss in the rice and stock and allow the mixture to boil. Lower the heat, cover the pan with lid and cook for 20 minutes. With the use of a fork fluff the rice.
8. Before you do anything set the oven to 375F.
9. Add the balance 1 tbsp of butter to a baking dish. Fold in the rice mixture to the baking dish and top up with the onion and sausage mixture.
10. Place the dish in the oven, loosely cover and leave for 22 minutes. Remove lid and bake for 12 minutes until heated through. Serve garnished with parsley.
11. Enjoy.

Paella
Brasileiro

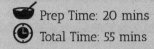 Prep Time: 20 mins

Total Time: 55 mins

Servings per Recipe: 8
Calories	527.3
Fat	17.4g
Cholesterol	156.3mg
Sodium	629.9mg
Carbohydrates	52.0g
Protein	38.4g

Ingredients

4 tbsp. olive oil
1 tbsp. garlic
3/4-1 lb. chicken breast, cut into pieces
1 large Spanish onion, diced
1 red bell pepper, diced
2 C. rice, short grain uncooked
2 tsps. oregano
1 pinch turmeric
2 lemons, zested
1 tbsp. paprika
1 tsp. crushed red pepper flakes
1 bay leaf
1 quart chicken stock
3/4-1 lb. pork, diced
3 - 4 roma tomatoes, chopped
1 C. green peas, frozen
1/2 bunch Italian parsley, chopped
3/4-1 lb. frozen cooked shrimp
salt & pepper

Directions

1. Wash the shrimp in running water to thaw and leave aside in a colander.
2. Pour olive oil into a skillet and heat well.
3. Sauté the garlic for 4 minutes.
4. Toss in the chicken, stir often and cook for 5 minutes.
5. Stir in red bell pepper and onion and allow to cook until the vegetables are soft and tender and the chicken is cooked through.
6. Fold in rice, stir often and toast the rice for 6 minutes.
7. Stir in turmeric, oregano, paprika, lemon zest and red pepper flakes to the chicken mixture and adjust seasonings.
8. Toss in bay leaf, sausage/pork/ham and chicken stock and combine well.
9. Lightly add the roma tomatoes.
10. Place lid and allow the mixture to simmer for 16 minutes on a reduced heat.
11. Check for salt and pepper and adjust as necessary.
12. Sprinkle parsley and green peas, place lid and allow to simmer for 6 minutes.
13. Add the precooked shrimp, cover with lid and leave to simmer for 8 minutes until warmed through.
14. Take out the bay leaf and discard.
15. Serve warm.
16. Enjoy.

HOW
to Make a Paella

Prep Time: 10 mins
Total Time: 55 mins

Servings per Recipe: 4
Calories	439.2
Fat	9.8g
Cholesterol	85.2mg
Sodium	1177.3mg
Carbohydrates	58.7g
Protein	29.8g

Ingredients

2 C. low sodium chicken broth
1/2 tsp. saffron thread
1 tbsp. olive oil
1 C. chopped onion
2/3 C. diced red bell pepper
2/3 C. diced green bell pepper
1/2 C. canned diced tomato, drained
1 tbsp. chopped garlic
1 tbsp. chopped fresh thyme

1 tsp. salt
1/2 tsp. ground black pepper
1 C. short-grain rice
1 C. frozen shelled edamame, thawed
1/2 lb. large shrimp, shelled and deveined
1/2 lb. sea scallops, halved
2 tbsp. chopped cilantro

Directions

1. Pour broth into a saucepan and heat well; remove from heat.
2. Stir in saffron and allow to sit for a few minutes.
3. Pour oil into a non-stick pan and heat well.
4. Sauté bell peppers and onion, keep covered, stir often and leave for 6 minutes. Stir in tomatoes, thyme, garlic, salt and pepper; combine well and cook for 4 minutes until the liquid is fully absorbed.
5. Fold in the rice; stir and cook for 2 minutes.
6. Pour broth over the rice and allow the mixture to boil.
7. Lower the heat, keep covered and allow to simmer for 16 minutes.
8. Stir in shrimp and scallops and edamame; keep covered and allow to simmer for 12 minutes until the seafood is cooked through.
9. Allow to stand for 6 minutes. Serve garnished with cilantro. Enjoy.

Paella Manila

🥣 Prep Time: 20 mins
🕐 Total Time: 50 mins

Servings per Recipe: 6
Calories   1141.7
Fat   74.6g
Cholesterol   221.0mg
Sodium   501.2mg
Carbohydrates   78.1g
Protein   43.8g

Ingredients

2 tbsp. peanut oil
1 onion, minced
2 garlic cloves, minced
2 green chilies, deseeded and chopped
1 medium chicken, chopped
2 C. chorizo sausage, sliced
2 tbsp. ginger, minced
1 C. glutinous rice, washed and drained
1 C. long grain rice, washed and drained
1/2 tsp. cayenne pepper

3 tsps. nam pla, crumbled
5 C. coconut milk
1 bay leaf
salt
2 red bell peppers, roasted, skinned and cut into strips
3 hard-boiled eggs, quartered

Directions

1. Pour oil into a skillet and heat well. Sauté the onions, chilies and garlic for 3 minutes.
2. Toss in the chicken and allow to cook until the meat is nicely browned on each side. Stir in ginger and chorizo and pan fry for 2 minutes. Then fold in the cayenne pepper and the rice.
3. Combine well and sauté for 2 minutes. Stir in the coconut milk and the nam pla and allow the mixture to boil. Fold in the bay leaf and combine well.
4. Reduce the heat and use an aluminum foil to cover. Place a lid on top of the aluminum foil and allow to simmer for 26 minutes.
5. Remove the cover and add seasonings. Spread the bell peppers on the surface of the rice and cover once again. Allow to rest for 6 minutes.
6. Serve garnished with hardboiled egg wedges. Enjoy.

10-MINUTE
Paella

Prep Time: 10 mins
Total Time: 10 mins

Servings per Recipe: 6
Calories	352.7
Fat	13.8g
Cholesterol	53.1m
Sodium	709.6mg
Carbohydrates	37.7g
Protein	18.9g

Ingredients

8 ounces boneless skinless chicken breasts, cut into pieces
8 ounces hot Italian sausages, sliced
1 medium onion, chopped
2 garlic cloves, minced
1 (19 ounce) cans stewed tomatoes, undrained
1 (10 ounce) cans chicken broth
1 medium green pepper, chopped

12 medium shrimp, cleaned
1/2 tsp. turmeric
2 C. Minute Rice, uncooked
1/2 C. frozen peas
3 tbsp. lemon juice, squeezed
2 tbsp. parsley, chopped

Directions

1. Place chicken, onions, sausage and garlic in a microwave safe dish and combine well.
2. Uncover and leave the dish in the microwave for 12 minutes on high; stir every 4 minutes.
3. Fold in chicken broth, tomatoes, peppers, turmeric, shrimp; combine well. Cover with lid and microwave for 7 minutes.
4. Stir in peas and Minute Rice; cover with lid and allow to sit for 12 minutes.
5. Drizzle lemon juice on top; serve garnished with parsley.
6. Enjoy.

Paella Carnival

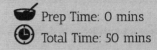 Prep Time: 0 mins
Total Time: 50 mins

Servings per Recipe: 6
Calories   900.4
Fat   57.1g
Cholesterol   141.7mg
Sodium   522.8mg
Carbohydrates   49.2g
Protein   43.5g

Ingredients

3/4 C. olive oil
2 1/2 lbs. chicken, boneless skinless breasts, cut into pieces
1 large onion, chopped
5 garlic cloves, minced
1 large green pepper, chopped
3 ounces dry sherry
1 1/2 C. rice, uncooked

3 C. chicken broth
1/4 tsp. saffron
1/4 tsp. turmeric
3 tbsp. fresh rosemary, chopped
3 large zucchini, strips
salt and pepper

Directions

1. Pour 1/4 C. of the olive oil into a skillet and heat well. Sauté the chicken until a nice brown in color on each side. Leave aside.
2. Clear the skillet, pour the balance olive oil and allow to heat. Toss in the onion and cook for 6 minutes.
3. Fold in the green pepper and garlic and cook for 4 minutes.
4. Pour the sherry over the ingredients and allow to cook for 2 minutes.
5. Fold in the rice and stir fry for 6 minutes.
6. Stir in the broth, turmeric, saffron, 1 1/2 tbsp of the rosemary and browned chicken and allow to cook for 16 minutes.
7. Sprinkle the balance rosemary on top and combine well.
8. Place the zucchini on top of the rice, cover with lid and allow to cook for 12 minutes more until the chicken is tender and the rice is cooked.
9. Leave to stand for 6 minutes; serve warm.
10. Enjoy.

SHORT
Grain Paella

Prep Time: 20 mins
Total Time: 1 hr 20 mins

Servings per Recipe: 8
Calories	651.9
Fat	21.4g
Cholesterol	104.6mg
Sodium	747.6mg
Carbohydrates	74.7g
Protein	36.7g

Ingredients

1/4 C. olive oil
1 lb. Spanish chorizo, sliced
1 onion, chopped
6 garlic cloves, minced
1/2 tbsp. saffron thread
1 tsp. turmeric
3 C. short-grain rice
3 C. chicken stock
2 C. green peas
1 lb. sea bass fillet, cut into 8 pieces
2 dozen cockles, scrubbed

1 lb. mussels, rinsed and debearded
18 large shrimp, peeled and deveined
1/2 lb. calamari, cleaned well and cut into rings
1 red pepper, roasted peeled and cut into strips
1/4 C. parsley, chopped
1 lemon, wedges

Directions

1. Pour the olive oil into a skillet and heat well; sauté the chorizo for 6 minutes. Lower the heat and fold in onions, saffron, garlic and turmeric and leave until the onions become soft for 9 minutes.

2. Fold in the rice and toast for 4 minutes. Pour the chicken stock over the ingredients, stir often and cook for 16 minutes; add more water if the mixture is too dry. Fold in the peas and baas into the rice; cook for 6 minutes until the fish becomes opaque.

3. Spread the clams or cockles in a platter. Place the hinges facing downward into the rice so then can open up; spread the mussels in the same manner. Flip the fish, spread the shrimp; lay the strips of pepper similar to wheel spokes. Allow to cook for 6 more minutes; flip the shrimp; lay the calamari. When the shells open up, dispose any unopened shells and seafood cooked through; sprinkle with parsley and serve garnished with wedges of lemon. Enjoy.

Sunday
Paella

 Prep Time: 10 mins

Total Time: 30 mins

Servings per Recipe: 5
Calories	140.4
Fat	3.5g
Cholesterol	58.7mg
Sodium	78.9mg
Carbohydrates	4.1g
Protein	22.0g

Ingredients

1 (10 ounce) packages saffron rice mix
1 tbsp. butter
2 1/2 C. water
1 -1 1/4 lb. boneless skinless chicken
breast
1/2 tsp. chopped garlic
cracked pepper
1/4 C. chopped onion

1/2 C. chopped bell pepper
1/2 C. peas

Directions

1. Rinse and dice the chicken into cubes.
2. Pour water into a pot and allow to boil. Stir in the rice mix and butter or olive oil.
3. Allow the mixture to cook for 2 minutes, cover with lid and lower the heat and allow the mixture to simmer.
4. Allow the rice to cook for 27 minutes.
5. In the meantime, use a cooking spray and spray a pan.
6. Sauté the garlic, chicken and cracked pepper for 12 minutes. The chicken should be not cooked through.
7. Stir in vegetables, cover with lid and allow to cook for further 12 minutes until the chicken is done.
8. Take out the vegetables and chicken from the pan and combine with the rice.
9. Enjoy.

HOT
Zucchini Paella

Prep Time: 15 mins
Total Time: 2 hrs 15 mins

Servings per Recipe: 4
Calories	407.6
Fat	8.6g
Cholesterol	0.0mg
Sodium	584.2mg
Carbohydrates	71.5g
Protein	10.6g

Ingredients

3 C. chicken broth
1 1/4 tsps. saffron threads
1 large red bell pepper, strips
1/2 lb. zucchini, sliced
2 tbsp. olive oil, divided
1 tsp. dried oregano
1 tsp. dried thyme
1 large onion, chopped
3 garlic cloves, chopped

1 jalapeno pepper, seeded and chopped
3 plum tomatoes, chopped
1 1/2 C. uncooked Arborio rice
lemon wedge

Directions

1. Add the saffron to the chicken broth and allow the mixture to boil, lower the heat and allow the mixture to simmer for 22 minutes.
2. Add the strips of bell pepper, 1 tbsp oil and zucchini and place them in a layer in a baking pan. Sprinkle thyme and oregano on top.
3. Place in the oven for 32 minutes at a temperature of 400F until the ingredients are tender, stir once.
4. Pour the balance 1 tbsp oil into a skillet and heat well. Pan fry the jalapeno and garlic in the hot oil for 27 minutes until the onion becomes caramelized.
5. Stir in tomatoes and leave for 6 minutes until the liquid becomes fully absorbed.
6. Toss in the rice and broth mixture in the skillet and allow the mixture to boil. Cover with lid, lower the heat and allow to simmer for 32 minutes, stir once after about 16 minutes.
7. Add zucchini and bell pepper and leave for 6 minutes.
8. Serve garnished with wedges of lemon. Enjoy.

Paella
Pilaf

 Prep Time: 30 mins
🕐 Total Time: 1 hr 15 mins

Servings per Recipe: 4
Calories	485.6
Fat	20.6g
Cholesterol	128.4mg
Sodium	1451.0mg
Carbohydrates	42.9g
Protein	29.3g

Ingredients

Pilaf
2 tbsp. onions
1 tbsp. butter
1 C. rice
2 C. water
2 tsps. salt
Paella
1/2 tsp. garlic powder
1/2 tsp. black pepper

1 pinch saffron threads
1/4 red pepper
1/4 green pepper
1/4-1/2 lb. shrimp, cleaned
1 lb. chicken
1/2 C. frozen peas
black olives

Directions

1. Mince the 2 tbsps. of onions. Place the butter or oil in a skillet with lid and heat well. Toss in rice and onions. Combine well and leave until the rice becomes a golden brown in color. Add salt and water and allow the mixture to boil. Cover with lid and cook on a reduced heat for 22 minutes until the rice becomes soft.
2. Dice the chicken into tiny pieces, clean, wash and dice the pepper into thin strips and cut the olives into slices.
3. Mix the chicken, spices, peppers and the rice mixture in a casserole dish. Place the dish in an oven for 22 minutes at a temperature of 350F.
4. Once the chicken is cooked, combine with frozen peas and shrimp.
5. Transfer back to the oven for 6 minutes.
6. Enjoy.

MY
First Paella

Prep Time: 20 mins
Total Time: 35 mins

Servings per Recipe: 2	
Calories	774.2
Fat	56.3g
Cholesterol	272.6mg
Sodium	2025.3mg
Carbohydrates	8.8g
Protein	54.7g

Ingredients

2/3 C. yellow rice
1 1/2 tbsp. olive oil
1 small shallot, chopped
1 garlic clove, minced
1/2 lb. large shrimp, shelled and deveined
1/2 lb. chorizo sausage, sliced
1 C. chicken broth

2 tbsp. chicken broth
1 tbsp. parsley, chopped
1/3 C. frozen peas

Directions

1. Pour olive oil into a skillet and heat well. Sauté the rice until a slight brown in color.
2. Toss in garlic and shallot and leave for 2 minutes.
3. Stir in chorizo, shrimp and broth. Cover with lid and cook for 20 minutes.
4. Take out the cover, stir in peas and parsley and cook until warm.
5. Continue to cook uncovered until the liquid is fully absorbed.
6. Enjoy..

No
Rice Paella

Prep Time: 15 mins
Total Time: 45 mins

Servings per Recipe: 4
Calories   454.6
Fat   100.2mg
Cholesterol   1451.0mg
Sodium   12.8g
Carbohydrates   33.6g
Protein

Ingredients

10 ounces chorizo sausage
2 boneless skinless chicken breasts, cut
into pieces
1 tsp. paprika
1 tsp. cumin
1/2 tsp. salt
1/2 tsp. pepper
1 medium onion, sliced
1 red pepper, sliced

1 large tomatoes, sliced
3 garlic cloves, minced
1 pinch saffron
1 C. chicken broth
1/2 head cauliflower, grated with box grater

Directions

1. Sauté the chorizo in a skillet until crisp. Transfer from the skillet leaving the pan drippings in the skillet.

2. Combine the chicken with cumin, paprika, salt and pepper. Sauté the chicken in pan drippings until done. Transfer from the pan and leave aside with chorizo.

3. Stir in onion and pepper and leave until the onions become soft. Toss in garlic and tomatoes and allow to cook, ensuring to remove any food items stuck to the bottom. Adjust seasonings with salt and pepper.

4. Stir in saffron and chicken broth and combine well. Allow the mixture to cook until the sauce is thick in consistency and the liquid is fully absorbed. Toss in the chicken, chorizo and cauliflower.

5. Cook for 6 minutes until the cauliflower becomes soft and tender.

6. Enjoy.

PAELLA
Dump Dinner

Prep Time: 15 mins
Total Time: 5 hrs 30 mins

Servings per Recipe: 4
Calories	317.7
Fat	3.9g
Cholesterol	72.9mg
Sodium	358.9mg
Carbohydrates	38.8g
Protein	30.5g

Ingredients

1 lb. boneless skinless chicken breast
1 (14 ounce) cans tomatoes, chopped
1 medium onion, chopped
1 medium bell pepper, chopped
1/2 C. canned chicken broth
3 medium garlic cloves, chopped
1 tsp. oregano
1 tsp. ground turmeric

1/2 tsp. thyme
1 dash Cajun seasoning
1/3 C. frozen green pea
2 C. cooked white rice

Directions

1. Dice the chicken into chunks.
2. Place the tomatoes, chicken, bell pepper, onion, seasonings and garlic in a slow cooker.
3. Cook for 5 hours on low.
4. Toss in the rice and peas and cook without lid for about 16 minutes until the peas are soft and tender.
5. Enjoy.

Alternative
European Paella

Prep Time: 5 mins
Total Time: 1 hr 05 mins

Servings per Recipe: 3
Calories	2255.4
Fat	114.2g
Cholesterol	655.0mg
Sodium	662.9mg
Carbohydrates	119.9g
Protein	166.4g

Ingredients

4 C. water
1/2 C. dry white wine
2 tbsp. black tea
1 tbsp. oil
1 C. snow peas
1 C. water chestnut
1 red chili
1 onion, chopped
2 C. rice

1 C. dried mango
1 kg chicken drumstick

Directions

1. Pour oil into a skillet and heat well. Sauté the chicken until cooked through.
2. Toss in the onions, mangoes, chili and combine well
3. Add rice, tea and 2 C. of water into the skillet and combine well.
4. Once the liquid is evaporated, stir in two C. and combine well.
5. When the mixture is dry, pour in the wine.
6. When the rice is cooked, stir in the water chestnuts and peas.
7. Combine the ingredients together and leave until the water chestnuts and peas are heated through.
8. Enjoy.

EASY
Orzo Paella

🥣 Prep Time: 15 mins
🕐 Total Time: 35 mins

Servings per Recipe: 6
Calories   326.4
Fat   9.5g
Cholesterol   38.1mg
Sodium   624.6mg
Carbohydrates   37.1g
Protein   23.4g

Ingredients

1 boneless chicken breast, cut into pieces
1 lb. Italian turkey sausage
1 large onion, diced small
1 red pepper, cut in thin strips
1 medium zucchini, diced small
1 (15 ounce) cans stewed tomatoes
2 C. water

sherry wine, just a splash
1/2 tsp. paprika
1 1/4 C. orzo pasta
1 tsp. oregano
salt and pepper

Directions

1. Take out the sausage from the casing and crumble into tiny pieces.
2. Place sausage and chicken in a skillet and allow to brown. Remove with a spatula.
3. Cook the onion, zucchini and red pepper in the skillet drippings until tender.
4. Stir in stewed tomatoes, 2 C. water, 1/2 tsp salt, orzo, paprika, oregano and meats.
5. Allow the mixture to boil.
6. Lower the heat and allow to simmer, keep covered whilst stirring once in a while for 22 minutes until the liquid is evaporated and the orzo becomes tender.
7. The orzo might stick to the bottom and you might have to use a flame-tamer under the skillet.
8. Enjoy.

Valencian
Paella

Prep Time: 1 hr
Total Time: 1 hr

Servings per Recipe: 1
Calories	1318.0
Fat	84.5g
Cholesterol	129.1mg
Sodium	965.8mg
Carbohydrates	93.3g
Protein	43.5g

Ingredients

1/2 C. uncooked valencian rice
1 C. chicken stock
5 saffron strands
4 tbsp. olive oil
1 piece chicken
1/2-1 soft chorizo sausage
1/2 tsp. Spanish sweet paprika
1 garlic clove, minced
1/4 C. chopped onion
1/8 C. grated tomatoes halved, grate & discard skin
2 prawns
2 - 4 small clams
2 - 4 small mussels
red pepper, strips
artichoke hearts,
green beans
cooked white Spanish beans
lemon wedge
salt

Directions

1. Pour stock in to a saucepan and heat well. Crumble the saffron and fold into the stock or a bit of white wine. Heat a skillet, pour olive oil and sauté chicken until nicely browned. Toss in onions and garlic and leave until soft.

2. Stir in chorizo and leave until heated through. Fold in the rice and combine well. Toss in the grated tomato and the paprika, stir and cook for a few minutes.

3. Pour in the saffron liquid and allow the mixture to boil; scrape off the bottom of the pan. Allow the mixture to simmer.

4. When the liquid has evaporated but still has an appearance of a soup, add the clams and mussels. Once the rice is done stir in the shrimp or prawns into the rice. Add the artichoke hearts, piquillo peppers, beans, green beans and peas.

5. The rice will caramelize and form a socarrat.

6. Leave aside to rest for 12 minutes. Sprinkle chopped parsley on top and garnish with wedges of lemon.

7. The oven or stove top could be used. Start the recipe on the stove top and then after stirring in the liquid transfer the pan in to a preheated oven of 400F.

8. Once the rice is cooked place on the stove top to form the caramelized crust.

9. Enjoy.

PAELLA
Beja

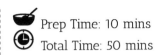 Prep Time: 10 mins
Total Time: 50 mins

Servings per Recipe: 6
Calories   286.3
Fat   7.1g
Cholesterol   81.8mg
Sodium   376.0mg
Carbohydrates   33.9g
Protein   20.4g

Ingredients

1 tbsp. olive oil
1/2 lb. chicken breast, cubed
1 C. uncooked rice
1 medium onion, chopped.
1 clove garlic, minced
1 1/2 C. chicken broth
1 (8 ounce) cans stewed tomatoes,
chopped, reserving liquid
1/2 tsp. paprika

1/8-1/4 tsp. ground red pepper
1/8 tsp. powdered saffron
1/2 lb. medium shrimp, peeled and
deveined
1 small red pepper, strips
1 small green pepper, strips
1/2 C. frozen green pea

Directions

1. If medium grain rice is being used, use 1 1/4 C. of broth, if parboiled rice is being used, use 1 3/4 C. of broth.
2. Pour oil into a skillet and heat well.
3. Sauté chicken until nicely browned.
4. Toss in rice, garlic and onion.
5. Allow to cook until the onion is soft and tender and rice is slightly browned.
6. Pour broth, tomato liquid, add tomatoes, ground red pepper, paprika and saffron.
7. Allow the mixture to boil and combine well.
8. Lower the heat; cover with lid and allow to simmer for 12 minutes.
9. Toss in shrimp, peas and strips of pepper, cover with lid and allow to simmer for 12 minutes until the liquid is evaporated and the rice becomes tender. Enjoy.

Country
Style Paella

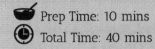 Prep Time: 10 mins

Total Time: 40 mins

Servings per Recipe: 4

Calories	184.5
Fat	4.9g
Cholesterol	86.8mg
Sodium	390.7mg
Carbohydrates	17.7g
Protein	17.5g

Ingredients

1 3/4 C. water

6 1/8 ounces original rice pilaf

1 tbsp. olive oil

1 tbsp. turmeric

1 tsp. hot pepper sauce

8 ounces medium shrimp, peeled and deveined

1 C. canned black beans, rinsed and drained

1 C. frozen peas

1 medium tomatoes, chopped

1 - 2 tbsp. chopped basil

Directions

1. Pour water into a pot and allow to boil. Fold in the rice, the spice sack, turmeric, olive oil and hot pepper sauce.

2. Cover with lid, lower the heat and allow the mixture to simmer for 12 minutes.

3. Fold in the shrimp, cover with lid and leave to simmer for further 16 minutes.

4. Stir in the black beans, tomato, peas and basil and leave for 6 more minutes to cook through.

5. Enjoy.

VEGETARIAN
Paella

Prep Time: 0 mins
Total Time: 52 mins

Servings per Recipe: 4
Calories   470.4
Fat   4.6g
Cholesterol   3.6mg
Sodium   338.9mg
Carbohydrates   95.8g
Protein   16.3g

Ingredients

1 1/2 C. brown rice
2 C. chicken stock
2 large onions, sliced
2 leeks, julienned
3 carrots, sliced
2 zucchini, sliced
2 garlic cloves, minced
1 red capsicum, sliced
2 tbsp. tomato paste

1 tsp. turmeric
4 tomatoes, peeled and chopped
ground black pepper
250 g broccoli, broken into florets
250 g cauliflower, broken into florets

Directions

1. Parboil the 1 1/2 C. of brown rice using the chicken stock or vegetable stock for 22 minutes. Leave aside without draining.
2. Stir in onions, carrots, leeks, garlic and zucchini to a pan and cook in 4 tbsp of water for 12 minutes.
3. Toss in pepper, turmeric, tomato paste and tomatoes and allow to cook for 3 minutes.
4. Fold in the parboiled rice and combine well and allow the mixture to simmer for 16 minutes.
5. Cook cauliflower and broccoli separately for 6 minutes and combine with the rice.
6. Enjoy.

Paella
South American

🥣 Prep Time: 2 hrs

🕐 Total Time: 3 hrs 40 mins

Servings per Recipe: 6

Calories	1060.6
Fat	38.3g
Cholesterol	261.8mg
Sodium	1198.8mg
Carbohydrates	99.4g
Protein	67.8g

Ingredients

2 1/2 C. medium grain rice
4 cloves garlic, minced
1 tsp. powdered saffron
1 lb. chicken breast, cubed
3 tomatoes, peeled, seeded and chopped
1 onion, chopped
8 ounces chorizo sausage, diced
1 C. cooked cannellini beans
1 C. cooked chickpeas
1 C. cooked chopped green beans
1 - 2 lb. clams
1 lb. shrimp, peeled and deveined
6 C. chicken stock
1 C. dry white wine
5 tbsp. olive oil

Directions

1. Rinse the canned beans, drain and leave aside.
2. Pour the chicken stock to a pan and allow the mixture to simmer. Stir in the saffron and allow to heat, or you could microwave on high for 7 minutes before adding to the pan.
3. Pour 1/4 C. of olive oil, heat well and sauté the chicken until nicely browned all over.
4. Transfer the chicken into a dish with kitchen towels for draining.
5. Add 1 tbsp oil and sauté the garlic, onions and tomato and leave for 32 minutes ensuring to stir frequently.
6. Place the chicken once again in the pan and combine well.
7. Pour 4 C. of the chicken stock and 1/2 C. of wine and allow to simmer for 6 minutes.
8. Add all the ingredients except the rice.
9. Combine well and try to place the clams in the bottom.
10. Stir in the rice and try to maintain the clams still at the bottom.
11. Cook for 35 minutes on high heat until the rice is cooked.
12. If the rice is still raw and the mixture dry, stir in 1/2 C. of stock and a dash of wine.
13. Allow the pan to stand for about 17 minutes until all the liquid is evaporated.
14. Dispose of any clams that don't open up and spread the balance on the top.
15. Enjoy.

TRADITIONAL
Long Grain Paella

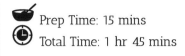
Prep Time: 15 mins

Total Time: 1 hr 45 mins

Servings per Recipe: 6

Calories	864.8
Fat	39.8g
Cholesterol	271.5mg
Sodium	808.3mg
Carbohydrates	46.0g
Protein	64.9g

Ingredients

4 whole chicken breasts, halved
salt & ground black pepper
1/4 C. butter, melted
1/4 tsp. coriander powder
1/3 C. cooking sherry
4 garlic cloves, minced
1 1/2 C. long-grain rice
1/3 C. Spanish olive oil
1 green pepper, strips
2 C. clam broth

1 C. chicken broth
1 lb. tomatoes, ripe, chopped
1/2 tsp. salt
1 1/2 tsp. sugar
1 lb. medium shrimp, shelled and deveined
1 dozen clam
1 dash cayenne pepper
3/4 C. pimento stuffed olive

Directions

1. Place the halved chicken breasts with skin side facing upwards in a casserole dish. Rub with salt, pepper and melted butter.
2. Sprinkle coriander on top, cover with aluminum foil and leave in the oven for 42 minutes at a temperature of 350F.
3. Remove the foil, drizzle sherry on top and bake for further 22 minutes. Baste once in a while with pan drippings.
4. Pour olive oil into a pan and heat well. Sauté the onion, garlic and rice until a light golden in color.
5. Toss in green pepper, tomatoes, broth, sugar and salt. Cover with lid and allow to simmer for 27 minutes, stirring once in a while.
6. Fold in chicken, clams, shrimp, olives and cayenne. Continue to cover and cook for 6 minutes until the clams open up and the liquid is evaporated. Enjoy..

Pasco
County Paella

Prep Time: 30 mins
Total Time: 1 hr 30 mins

Servings per Recipe: 8
Calories   635.9
Fat   17.0g
Cholesterol   109.3mg
Sodium   1091.8mg
Carbohydrates   68.8g
Protein   42.2g

Ingredients

6 boneless skinless chicken breasts
3 chorizo sausage, sliced
18 large shrimp, shelled & deveined
1 lb. mussels
2 tbsp. olive oil
5 C. chicken broth
1 C. white wine
1 pinch saffron

1 onion, chopped
3 garlic cloves, chopped
salt, pepper, paprika
1 C. peas
1 (4 ounce) jars pimientos
3 C. Arborio rice

Directions

1. Before you do anything set the oven to 400F.
2. Pour 1 tbsp oil into a pan and pan fry the chorizo. Remove the chorizo and leave aside.
3. Pour more oil into the pan, sauté chicken on all sides and remove.
4. Heat saffron and chicken broth and leave aside.
5. Pour oil, add onions and garlic and pan fry until onions become soft. Stir in rice and allow to coat evenly with the oil.
6. Pour wine and broth, combine and add spices. Allow the mixture to boil and keep stirring frequently.
7. Allow the liquid to reduce, stir in peas and pimentos.
8. Toss in chicken and chorizo and combine well.
9. Place in the preheated oven, keep uncovered for 12 minutes.
10. Place mussels and shrimp, combine and heat for 12 minutes until the liquid has evaporated.
11. Serve garnished with parsley.
12. Enjoy.

PAELLA
to Share

🥣 Prep Time: 25 mins
🕐 Total Time: 45 mins

Servings per Recipe: 2	
Calories	1136.6
Fat	22.7g
Cholesterol	196.7mg
Sodium	481.1mg
Carbohydrates	171.8g
Protein	50.5g

Ingredients

1 1/2 tbsp. vegetable oil
Long Grain
1/4 C. carrot, diced
1/4 C. white onion, diced
1/4 C. red bell pepper, diced
1/2 tbsp. garlic, minced
1 pinch saffron
4 bay leaves
2 C. long grain rice
olive oil
chicken stock
Paella
4 slices hot Italian sausage
4 ounces chicken pieces
4 shrimp, with head on, unpeeled
2 ounces lobster meat
2 ounces fish

2 ounces sliced calamari, tentacles kept whole
8 mussels
4 frozen whole cooked crawfish
salt & ground pepper
1 dash habanero sauce
1 sprig thyme
1/4 C. white wine
1/4 C. frozen peas
2 leeks, sliced
red pepper, sliced
lemon wedge
cilantro, sliced

Directions

1. Pour vegetable oil into a skillet and heat well. Sauté the onion, carrot and pepper for 2 minutes. Toss in the saffron, garlic, bay leaves and add the rice.
2. Combine the ingredients well, add a bit of olive oil to evenly coat the rice and leave until the rice is tender.
3. Pour chicken stock to cover the rice by about 1". Cover with lid and allow to simmer.
4. Take out the rice from the skillet and lay on a parchment sheet to stop the rice from cooking.

5. Before you do anything set the oven to 400F. In a separate skillet stir fry the chicken and sausage and allow to brown; then stir in the shrimp, fish, lobster, mussels, calamari and crawfish.

6. Stir fry for a few minutes; fold in the habanera hot sauce, salt, pepper, white wine and thyme.

7. Enjoy.

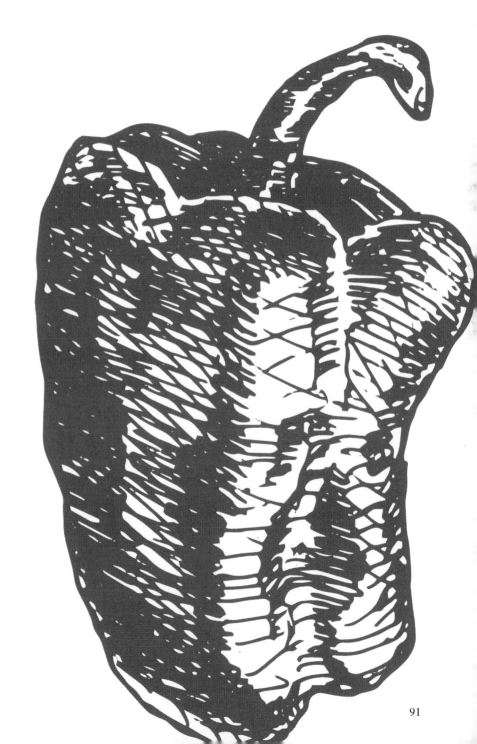

LOS ANGELES
Taco Paella

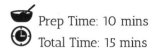
Prep Time: 10 mins
Total Time: 15 mins

Servings per Recipe: 2
Calories	4361.7
Fat	288.9 g
Cholesterol	264.8mg
Sodium	2803.0mg
Carbohydrates	333.4g
Protein	116.4g

Ingredients

6 - 9 six inch flour tortillas
2 - 3 C. Spanish-flavor couscous
1 (10 ounce) cans kidney beans
6 leaves iceberg lettuce
8 cherry tomatoes
6 black olives
1 avocado
1 C. shredded cheddar cheese
1/2 C. sour cream
1/2 C. salsa
1 lb. 2 tbsp. olive oil
1 skinless chicken breast, cubed
20 frozen shrimp, defrosted and shells removed
1/2 C. spicy sausage, sliced

1/2 medium onion, diced
1/2 C. frozen julienned bell pepper
1 tbsp. minced garlic paste
1 tsp. ground turmeric
1 tsp. white pepper
1 tsp. oregano flakes
1 tsp. dried thyme
1 tbsp. cayenne pepper
1 tsp. paprika
1 1/4 C. chicken stock
1 (15 ounce) cans diced tomatoes with juice
1 1/4 C. couscous
snipped parsley

Directions

1. Combine the kidney beans and the leftover paella, cover with lid and leave in the microwave for 4 minutes.
2. In the meantime, cut the lettuce, black olives, tomatoes and avocado into slices.
3. Spread each ingredient in individual serving dishes.
4. Place shredded cheddar cheese, sour cream and salsa in individual serving dishes.
5. Take out the heated paella from the microwave and place in a platter.
6. Place kitchen towel to cover the tortillas and heat in the microwave.
7. Place the platter on the pantry top and fill the tortilla using the available ingredients.
8. Enjoy

Paella Marrakesh

🥣 Prep Time: 15 mins

🕐 Total Time: 30 mins

Servings per Recipe: 4

Calories	474.8
Fat	22.1g
Cholesterol	78.5mg
Sodium	449.1mg
Carbohydrates	49.2g
Protein	21.9g

Ingredients

1 tbsp. vegetable oil
1/2 C. red bell pepper, chopped
4 scallions, chopped
2 garlic cloves, minced
1 tsp. coriander, ground
1/2 tsp. turmeric
1 pinch cayenne
2 C. vegetable stock, hot
225 g prawns, shelled pre-cooked, cubed
1 C. peas, fresh or frozen

1 C. couscous
1 tbsp. butter
100 g almonds, flaked and toasted
salt and pepper
parsley, chopped
lemon wedge

Directions

1. Pour oil into a skillet and heat well. Sauté the peppers, garlic, scallions, cayenne, coriander and turmeric for 5 minutes ensuring to stir occasionally.

2. Pour the stock or water into the skillet. Toss in the shrimp and leave for further 5 minutes until the shrimp turns pink in color. Fold in the peas and leave for another 2 minutes.

3. Stir in the couscous and margarine or butter. Cover with lid, transfer from heat and allow to stand for 6 minutes.

4. Remove the lid from the skillet, use a fork to botch the couscous to break up any chunks.

5. Adjust seasonings with salt and pepper. Top up with toasted almonds, lemon wedges and parsley and serve on a plate.

6. Enjoy.

HOT
Tropical Paella

Prep Time: 10 mins
Total Time: 25 mins

Servings per Recipe: 1
Calories   1766.3
Fat   44.1g
Cholesterol   0.0mg
Sodium   3371.4mg
Carbohydrates   329.6g
Protein   52.4g

Ingredients

15 scotch bonnet peppers
1 ripe mango
1/2 C. mustard powder
1 tsp. salt
1/2 C. brown sugar
1/2 C. white wine vinegar
1 tbsp. curry powder

1 tbsp. chili powder
1 tbsp. ground cumin
1 tbsp. ground ginger
1/2 tsp. ground star anise

Directions

1. Rinse the peppers and take off the stalks.
2. Remove the skin from the mango and deseed.
3. Heat the chilies for 7 minutes and place them in a food processor with the rest of the ingredients and process well.
4. If the sauce is too thick in consistency add more white wine vinegar.
5. Once blending is completed place the mixture in a pot, allow the mixture to boil and then simmer for 9 minutes.
6. Place the mixture in a heatproof container and seal.
7. Can be kept for a few months in the refrigerator.
8. Enjoy.

Portuguese
One Pot

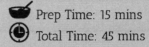 Prep Time: 15 mins

Total Time: 45 mins

Servings per Recipe: 6
Calories	1564.7
Fat	47.4g
Cholesterol	78.4mg
Sodium	1294.4mg
Carbohydrates	229.2g
Protein	48.9g

Ingredients

1/2 rabbit, chopped
1 chicken thigh, chopped
1 lb. rib, chopped
1 kg broad bean, broken into pieces
2 liters boiling chicken stock
750 g of round grain rice
5 garlic cloves

2 red peppers
4 tbsp. olive oil
3 tbsp. olive oil

Directions

1. Pour oil into a skillet and heat well. Add garlic and sauté and leave for a few minutes. Stir in the green beans and combine with a wooden spatula.
2. Leave the beans for 3 minutes in the skillet and move them to the side of the skillet.
3. Add the rice to the center of the pan and leave for 2 minutes.
4. With the use of the wooden spatula combine with rice and beans and lay evenly in the skillet.
5. Pour the chicken stock into the rice.
6. Stir in the chopped meat into the hot chicken stock and the rice mixture,
7. Spread the paprika strips on top and decorate the rice.
8. Allow the chicken stock to reduce and the rice to cook. Once the rice is cooked take the skillet off from the heat and use newspaper to cover the skillet.
9. Allow the paella to rest for 6 minutes.
10. Enjoy.

MEDITERRANEAN
Paella

Prep Time: 25 mins
Total Time: 1 hr 25 mins

Servings per Recipe: 8

Calories	814
Fat	38.1
Cholesterol	98
Sodium	1150
Carbohydrates	80.1
Protein	37.4

Ingredients

4 C. chicken stock
20 saffron threads, crushed
3/4 C. olive oil
4 chicken thighs
1 C. chopped onion
4 cloves garlic, minced
4 links spicy Spanish semi-cured sausage
2 C. Spanish paella rice
2 tsps. Spanish sweet paprika
1/2 C. grated peeled roma tomatoes
8 clams in shell, scrubbed, or more
8 mussels, cleaned and debearded
8 prawns, peeled and deveined
3 red bell peppers, cut into strips
10 ounces peas
salt and ground black pepper
1/2 C. chopped fresh Italian parsley
8 wedges lemon
1 baguette, sliced

Directions

1. Pour the stock into a saucepan and heat well. Add saffron into the hot stock.

2. Pour olive oil into a skillet and heat well. Sauté the chicken pieces for 6 minutes on each side until a slight brown in color. Toss in garlic and onion and cook for 8 minutes until the onion becomes tender. Lay the sausage around the chicken into the skillet and cook for 6 minutes on each side.

3. Fold in the rice into the skillet and allow to coat with the olive oil; adjust seasonings by adding paprika. Add the tomato and cook for 4 minutes.

4. Drizzle the chicken stock into the skillet and allow the mixture to boil. Ensure to scrape off any food stuck to the bottom of the skillet. Flatten the rice mixture with the use of a wooden spatula.

5. Lower the heat; continue cooking without combining until the rice becomes soft for about 35 minutes.

6. Fold in the mussels and clams with hinged side facing downwards on the rice; continue to cook until the clams and mussels open for 8 minutes.

7. Add the prawns, peas and bell pepper into

the rice. Cook the rice until fragrant for about 12 minutes. Transfer from heat and allow to cool for 12 minutes. Adjust seasonings by adding salt and pepper. Serve garnished with chopped parsley and wedges of lemon. Can be served with slices of baguette.

8. Enjoy.

Printed in Great Britain
by Amazon

69100526R00056